BISON
BOOKS

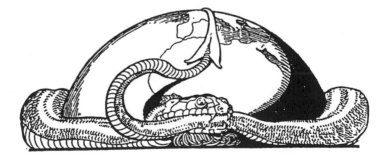

One of many depictions of the "mystic serpent," described in the most important published version of the *Protocols of the Elders of Zion*. The tail lodged in its own fangs signified that the monster's path through history and across the world had been completed: Jewry, in the form of the Antichrist, now ruled the earth. From Gottfried zur Beek [Ludwig Müller von Hausen], *Die Geheimnisse der Weisen von Zion* (1920).

Binjamin W. Segel

A LIE AND A LIBEL

The History of the *Protocols of the Elders of Zion*

Richard S. Levy, Translator and Editor

University of Nebraska Press, Lincoln and London

Welt-Krieg, Welt-Revolution, Welt-Verschwörung, Welt-Oberregierung © 1926 Translation © 1995 by the University of Nebraska Press All rights reserved Manufactured in the United States of America   The paper in this book meets the minimum requirements of American National Standard for Information Sciences – Permanence of Paper for Printed Library Materials, ANSI Z39.48-1984. Second cloth printing 1996. First Bison Books printing 1996. Most recent printing indicated by the last digit following: 10   9   8   7   6   5   4   3   2   1   Library of Congress Cataloging-in-Publication Data Segel, B. W. [Welt-Krieg, Welt-Revolution, Welt-Verschwörung, Welt-Oberregierung, English] A lie and a libel: the history of the Protocols of the Elders of Zion / Binjamin W. Segel; Richard S. Levy, translator & editor.

    p.   cm. Includes bibliographical references and index.

    ISBN 0-8032-4243-3 (cl.) ISBN 0-8032-9245-7 (pa.) 1. Protocols of the wise men of Zion. 2. Antisemitism – History. I. Levy, Richard S. II. Protocols of the wise men of Zion. III. Title.

    DS145.P7S43   1996   305.892′4 – dc20   95-10034 CIP

For Linnea

CONTENTS

PREFACE

Binjamin W. Segel's critique of the *Protocols of the Elders of Zion* stands on its own and deserves to be known by a wider public. Intelligent readers need to be educated about the contents of the *Protocols* and the historical and present-day political influence of this thoroughly libelous and mean-spirited forgery. Sad to say, however, the editor and publisher of Segel's critique had misgivings about providing a handy new edition of the *Protocols* itself. Segel's study in a new translation, along with an introduction that places the *Protocols* in a larger and more up-to-date context, it is hoped, will answer the needs of legitimate students. A brief excerpt from the *Protocols* text itself is reproduced here to contribute to readers' understanding, but it will be of little use to those who would circulate the *Protocols* for the usual destructive purposes.

NOTE ON THE TRANSLATION
Segel wrote two books on the subject of the *Protocols,* a long, scholarly study entitled *Die Protokolle der Weisen von Zion, kritisch beleuchtet* (The Protocols of the Elders of Zion, critically illuminated; Berlin, 1924) and the shorter, *Welt-Krieg, Welt-Revolution, Welt-Verschwörung, Welt-Oberregierung* (World war, world revolution, world conspiracy, world supergovernment; Berlin, 1926). It is the abbreviated version that is translated here.

In his attempt to reach the widest possible audience, Segel made several compromises in this version. He sharply reduced the number of illustrative examples and textual comparisons; he also eliminated much of the scholarly apparatus. One choice he made is somewhat problematical for the translator. To seize and hold his readers' attention, Segel begins his treatment with an overview of the subject. He then traverses the same ground in greater detail, sometimes with word-for-word repetitions. In the following translation, I have retained his format while eliminating several repetitions, in some places through amalgamation, in others through rearrangement. For the sake of accuracy, and because Segel's work is a document of historical interest in itself, I have refrained from excessive tampering.

Endnotes are provided to explain references to events and personalities that, while known to Segel's readers, are no longer familiar. Parenthetical statements are part of the original text; those in square brackets are mine.

Finally, a word on usage. The terms *antisemite* and *antisemitism* are used throughout to counter the false impression perpetuated by the common practice of capitalizing the root in the resulting compounds, *anti-Semite* and *anti-Semitism*. *Anti-Semitism* is not only a misnomer — it does not apply to the majority of Semites, that is, the Arab peoples — but it also gives continued life to a pernicious myth. "Semitism," a collection of exclusively negative traits comprising a monolithic Jewish essence, existed only in the minds of the enemies of Jews. Jews and their allies who opposed the antisemites were defending not this imaginary "Semitism" but their human rights.

Once again, Jonathan Marwil, David Jordan, John Kulczycki, and Robert Melson have given me the benefit of their friendship and wisdom, both of which I value beyond words. I would like also to thank here Sharon Ihnen, whose careful reading of the manuscript much improved it. All their help and constructive criticism notwithstanding, any shortcomings that remain are my own responsibility.

Richard S. Levy
University of Illinois at Chicago

A CHRONOLOGY

OF THE *PROTOCOLS*

1897–1899
Most likely date for fabrication of the *Protocols* in Paris, supervised by Pyotr Ivanovich Rachkovsky, the head of the Russian secret police (Okhrana) abroad.

1903, 26 August–3 September
Earliest known publication of the *Protocols* in abbreviated form, by Pavolachi Krushevan in his Russian-language newspaper, *Znamia* (The banner).

1905
Sergei Nilus (1862–1930) publishes the longer version, on which most subsequent editions draw, as an appendix to the second edition of his book *Velikoe v Malom* (*The Great in the Small*; Tsarskoe Selo, 1905).

1906
G. Butmi publishes a third version of the *Protocols* in his *Vragi Roda Chelovecheskago* (Enemies of the human race; 3d and 4th eds., St. Petersburg, 1906–7).

1911–1912
Nilus publishes the *Protocols* for the second and third times.

1917
In his fourth publication of the *Protocols,* Nilus attributes them for the first time to Theodor Herzl.

1919 January
Typescript copies of the *Protocols* distributed by anti-Bolshevik
White Russian émigrés at the Versailles Peace Conference, and to
members of the U.S. cabinet, judiciary, and intelligence agencies of
the army and navy.

1920
Russian-language editions published in Berlin, New York, Paris,
and Tokyo (1920–22).

Gottfried zur Beek (Ludwig Müller von Hausen, 1851–1929) publishes the *Protocols* in German, the first non-Russian version (dated
1919; in fact mid-January 1920). Thirty-three editions by 1933.

Henry Ford's weekly *Dearborn Independent* devotes lead articles to
the "Jewish World conspiracy," drawing freely from the *Protocols*
(22 May–2 Oct 1920). *The Protocols and World Revolution,* a White
Russian adaptation, appears in Boston (1920).

In Great Britain, the *Protocols* is published in January 1920 under the
title *The Jewish Peril.* The *Times* of London deals with the book on
8 May: "A Disturbing Pamphlet: a Call for Enquiry." London's
Morning Post features a series of eighteen articles (summer 1920)
entitled *The Cause of World Unrest.* A new translation of the *Protocols*
by one of the *Morning Post*'s reporters, Victor Marsden, is published
by the antisemitic organization known as the Britons. It becomes
the standard English-language edition.

First of eight French translations appears (the last in 1938). The
antisemitic daily *La Libre Parole* serializes the complete *Protocols.*

Four versions circulate in Poland (1920–34). Émigré Poles in
America produce a Polish-language edition (1920) for distribution
in North and South America.

1921
First Arabic translation, Damascus. First Italian translation.

Philip Graves, reporter for the *Times* of London, makes the connection between the *Protocols* and its major source, Maurice Joly's satire

of Napoleon III, *Dialogue between Machiavelli and Montesquieu in Hell* (Brussels, 1864). Graves debunks the forgery in the *Times* (16–18 August) in a lead article, "The End of the Protocols."

1922
Henry Ford publishes *The International Jew: The World's Foremost Problem* (reprint of the articles from his newspaper).

1923
Theodor Fritsch brings out a new German version (his second) based on the English translation; sells 100,000 copies by 1933.

Alfred Rosenberg, "official" philosopher of the Nazi Party, writes *The Protocols of the Elders of Zion and Jewish World Policy,* reprinted three times within a year.

1927, 30 June
Henry Ford publicly retracts and apologizes for *The International Jew,* claiming to have been duped by his assistants. Fritsch continues publishing it in Germany.

1929
The Nazi Party obtains the rights to zur Beek's translation.

1933
Excerpts from the *Protocols* read into the minutes of the Romanian parliament and used by native Fascists to demand the expulsion of Jews from the country.

1934–1937
In Port Elizabeth, South Africa, the *Protocols* goes on trial and is declared a forgery. The court in Bern, Switzerland, finds the book to be a fraudulent plagiarism of Joly's book.

1936–1937
Portuguese-language translations appear in Brazil.

1939
3 November
Hitler suggests distribution of the *Protocols* abroad to demonstrate that the true instigators of the war are Jews and Freemasons.

29 December
Spanish Falangists publish the *Protocols* as a prelude to Franco's New Years's denunciation of Jews and Freemasons.

1957–1959
Brutukul Hukama' Sahyun (The Protocols of the Elders of Zion) and *al-Shuyu 'iyya wa-al Sahyuniyya* (Communism and Zionism) appear in Egypt in the aftermath of the Suez campaign.

1964
Deluxe edition published in Spain.

1967, August
"What Is Zionism?", an article appearing in *Pravda* and hundreds of provincial newspapers on the same day, launches the Soviet anti-"Zionist" campaign, repeating many of the charges made in the *Protocols*.

1968
The Islamic Institute in Beirut produces 300,000 copies of the *Protocols* in French, Italian, Spanish, and Arabic.

1972
In Spain, a paperback edition of the *Protocols* "explains" the Catholic Church reforms of Vatican II.

In Italy, a new edition appears under the auspices of the neo-Fascist *Ordino Nuovo*.

Los Protocolos de los Sabios de Sion y la Subversion Mundial figures in the "Andinia plot," an alleged "Zionist" attempt to found a Jewish state in Argentina.

1974
Protocols published in Bombay under the title *International Conspiracy against Indians*.

1977
The *Thunderbolt,* newspaper of the National States Rights Party, advertises three separate editions of the *Protocols,* including the "super-large" version with commentary by Henry Ford.

1987
Yudayajin to Kuremurin: futatsu no Giteisho, the first edition of the *Protocols* in Japanese.

1992
Pamyat, a Russian extremist group, publishes the *Protocols*.

1994
Australian edition produced by Christian fundamentalists.

Masons, Jews, and Revolutions: How These Forces of Satan Are Preparing the End of Mankind, a rehash of the *Protocols,* published in Bulgaria.

INTRODUCTION

THE POLITICAL CAREER OF THE
PROTOCOLS OF THE ELDERS OF
ZION

Richard S. Levy

The *Protocols of the Elders of Zion,* one of the most important forgeries of modern times, presents a Jewish plot to take over the world and to reduce non-Jews to abject slavery. Created in Paris at the turn of the century, the document surfaced in Russia a few years later as part of a larger book. Thereafter, although published under many different titles, the forgery retained its essential character as a slapdash patchwork composed of several earlier, unrelated writings: a political satire of the mid–nineteenth century that had nothing to do with Jews; a trashy novel of the same period; and a well-developed strain of anti-Masonic literature. Despite such unpromising beginnings, the *Protocols* found a huge audience, especially in the turbulent times following World War I and then again during the Great Depression of the 1930s. Translated into every major European language, as well as Turkish, Japanese, Chinese, and Arabic, the work continues to appear and reappear throughout the world.

Why has the *Protocols of the Elders of Zion,* a shameless fraud, seized the imagination and informed the political judgment of men and women throughout the twentieth century? Attempting to answer this question has engaged the best efforts of statesmen, historians, philosophers, psychologists, and men of letters. Their task has been all the more daunting because the patent absurdity of the scheme has had little or no bearing on its credibility for a large and varied public. Indeed, almost as soon as the *Protocols* assumed political significance in the 1920s, analyses such as the following one by

Binjamin W. Segel subjected the work to mercilessly rational scrutiny. Critics swiftly discovered the book's plagiarized sources, exposed its faulty logic, laid bare its political motives, and condemned its defiance of common sense. For seventy-five years, Jews and non-Jews, churchmen, politicians, and private citizens of nearly every persuasion and from nearly every country where the *Protocols* has appeared have ridiculed it as a blatant hoax. Yet devastating and authoritative judgments have failed to put an end to the book. It still turns up in likely and unlikely places all over the world.

On first reading the *Protocols of the Elders of Zion* today, the student may be inclined to think that he or she is dealing with a clumsy, none-too-humorous satire. The depiction of a two-thousand-year-old, arcanely elaborated Jewish conspiracy, possessed of an astounding intelligence network and directed by a committee of nameless but bloodthirsty individuals immune to every decent human impulse, will strike most readers as wholly ludicrous. The claim that the fictitious "Elders of Zion" already stage-manage world events and are near final victory will alarm few people open to reason. But the *Protocols of the Elders of Zion* is not satire, and its durability has nothing to do with reasonableness. As this brief sketch of the book's political career will show, some people are willing to find the work credible, and others gladly exploit that willingness.

Readers of the *Protocols* may be inclined to shake their heads in either dismay or amusement at yet another proof of the gullibility of the great public. We live, after all, in the age of the tabloids, both print and television versions, where ordinary citizens take jaunts on alien spaceships and others go on an "all-pizza diet," expecting immediate weight loss. Such pandering to a person's lack of good sense, however, seems relatively innocent when compared with the purposeful uses of the *Protocols of the Elders of Zion*. From its first publication in 1903, the book was meant to serve a political function, to influence powerful individuals or mobilize large groups of people to think or act in particularly destructive and self-deluding ways. Over time, the political agendas of the publishers of the *Protocols* have changed, but the sowing of hatred and the urge to self-defense against the "enemy of mankind" have remained common to them all. This is not innocent literature.

Although one might expect the *Protocols* to raise the gravest doubts in readers, no matter the degree of their sophistication, the book clearly does not always do so. In the 1920s and 1930s, a significant number of people in all social strata believed in the authenticity of the document and took its revelation of a worldwide Jewish conspiracy at face value. They found in its pages a credible explanation of world events and spoke seriously of the "Jewish peril." Such is still the case in certain areas of the world in the 1990s. This being so, we would be mistaken to dismiss the *Protocols* as arrant nonsense. We ought, instead, to consider the reasons why the book has survived to the present day and examine the sources from which it draws strength.

§

The *Protocols* combines two distinct motifs: the conspiratorial and the antisemitic. In the twentieth century both are familiar and both have peculiar appeal for particular, although not necessarily identical, audiences. Segel gives considerable attention to the first of these motifs by way of putting the *Protocols* into its proper historical context. But his contempt for the conspiratorial mode of theorizing about historical events leads him to underestimate its allure for even the well educated. Conspiracy thinking was not then and is not now exclusively the property of the weak-minded, the deranged, or the semieducated. The dark doings of secret societies figured in the great nineteenth-century novels of Goethe, Scott, Balzac, Dickens, and Disraeli, in the grand operas of Mozart and Verdi, in the gothic romance, and in many other vehicles of both popular and high culture. The fascination with conspiracy themes lives on in the modern thriller and the caper film, entertainments with their own broadly based appeal.

For most people, conspiracy remains a recreational or aesthetic consideration. But on occasion and for even the highly intelligent and well educated, conspiracies explain the real world. Since the English Revolution of the seventeenth century and the French Revolution of the eighteenth, conspiracy has frequently been seen as the best explanation of real events. Jesuits and Jacobins, Wobblies and eastern bankers, suffragettes and misogynists have all, at one time or another, been endowed with both the power and the motive to control the unfolding of history. In our own day, the number, depth, and breadth of conspiracy theories spun to explain the assassination of John F. Kennedy should convince us of the continuing viability of this mode of thought. When seen in this context, an understanding of how the *Protocols* penetrated into literate circles becomes easier. The idea that sinister forces could control our lives from behind the scenes did not destroy but rather enhanced the credibility of the "Elders of Zion."

For many, the least likely explanation of great events seems the best because it is also the most effortless. Painstaking study of the data is not the strength of such people. Examining structural shifts in the economy, demographic trends, and sociological changes or making fine distinctions among life's complexities — all such undertakings demand serious work and rigorous thinking. By contrast, accepting the existence of a conspiracy provides the believer with a shortcut to "the cause" of the evil in question; he or she has but to fill in the details, make the obscure connections, reveal the intricacies of the plot. This is the kind of ingenuity many possess and enjoy exercising, and it is exactly what causes Segel to raise objections.

But the appeal of conspiracy thinking has to do not only with mental laziness or aesthetic pleasure. An investigation of disturbing public happenings that is carried out with respect for the laws of evidence often reaches no satisfactory conclusion. To many caught up in the numerous crises of modern times, such a lack of certainty is psychologically unacceptable. Offered a simple and dramatic version of politics, they seize it because even truly terrifying answers are preferable to gnawing uncertainty. The *Protocols of the Elders of Zion* exploits this all-too-human need in an unoriginal, yet powerful, manner.

Typical of the genre, the *Protocols* portrays a community unaware of the true laws of its own existence. Thinking itself autonomous and self-regulating, it is, in fact, being ruled by a secret society of evil men who have access to a global network of operatives. This society, which has origins deep in the past, has never wavered in its aims: the overthrow of the fundamental institutions, values, and traditions of the community. The cabal is infinitely flexible in the means it chooses, but it always uses unwitting agents from within the community itself to further the gradual process of destruction. Spreading discontent among the naive, sowing moral corruption in the young, turning class against class, the conspirators work their will on the hapless victims.[1]

The *Protocols* goads the "victims" of conspiracy into rage, hoping perhaps that they will retaliate against their oppressors. But the book appeals to its audience in more subtle ways as well. Those who wrote the long, appreciative commentaries that usually accompany the *Protocols* invite readers to join the elite of those "in the know." They are offered the veritable Rosetta stone of history, the single key that unlocks all the perplexing mysteries of the modern world. After being enlightened by this document, readers will rise above the helpless ignorance that characterizes the majority of their unsuspecting compatriots. Although the prospect of imminent Jewish triumph might be horrifying, knowledge of the conspiracy, as Hitler promised in *Mein Kampf,* would render it conquerable. The *Protocols* continues to hold out this hope to frightened, angry people.

The *Protocols of the Elders of Zion* also draws strength from another well-established tradition. The body of ideas about Jews and the ever-changing suggestions about what ought to be done with them was already enormous by the late 1890s, when the *Protocols* was fabricated. Segel refers to this only in passing, as an explanation of how Jews came to be numbered among the conspirators responsible for previous revolutions. However, the antisemitic tradition deserves greater attention.[2]

Antisemitism, a word coined in 1879 in Germany, differed significantly from the anti-Jewish hostility that preceded it by centuries. Jews living in European lands and in those parts of the world where Europeans settled had gradually become a pariah people — the embodiment of evil instincts, a false religion, and inferior physical traits. Until the late eighteenth century, with few exceptions they lived apart, wrapped in their own self-sufficient religious culture, subject to severe legal disabilities, special taxes, occasional expulsion, and outbursts of popular fury. Although much on the minds of other peoples, Jews were left to themselves for long periods. Their only connection to the larger societies in which they lived was in the economic sphere, where a few amassed legendary fortunes while the great majority pursued marginal, "obnoxious" occupations, such as moneylending, peddling, rent collecting, and tavern keeping.

Only after Jews had begun to emerge from their isolation did antisemitism begin to surface in Europe. Instead of episodic repression and violence, followed by decades of calm, antisemites endeavored to make persecution of the Jews permanent. Convinced that Jews had already gathered enormous power and that, as one pamphlet of the time put it, "the victory of Jewry" was imminent, antisemites determined that constant struggle against the enemy was an absolute necessity for the survival of "Christian civilization." They founded political parties, voluntary associations, newspapers, and periodicals to this end. In the last quarter of the nineteenth century, the word *antisemitism* expressed a new way of dealing with the "problem of the Jews."

This is a different order of thinking than is apparent in the literature of conspiracy. Historically, there actually were secret societies engaged in behind-the-scenes political activity; they have left documentary evidence of their existence. Although lacking the enormous power attributed to them by their would-be unmaskers, such societies were not wholly imaginary. As much cannot be said of the claim that a monolithic Jewry is engaged in a conspiracy of world conquest. For this fantasy there is not and has never been any evidence.

The creators of antisemitic ideology and the practitioners of antisemitic politics saw it otherwise. What persuaded the loose collection of Christian conservatives, former democrats and liberals, frustrated intellectuals, and career failures, as well as some eminent public figures, to devote their energies to combating the Jews was the granting of Jewish emancipation.

The struggle of Jews to get free of formal legal and social prohibitions, to join the mainstream of European life, began in the mid-eighteenth century. It took nearly a hundred years to realize, in some places considerably longer. Even then, emancipation usually remained at best only partial, more a theoretical than a practical reality, as Segel puts it. Because they were an essentially powerless minority everywhere, Jews had need of allies in their fight for equality. They found supporters among those with progressive political views, as Jewish emancipation merged almost imperceptibly with the more general movement toward bourgeois liberation from aristocratic and monarchical domination. The French Revolution of 1789 and the European-wide revolutions of 1848 hastened Jewish emancipation and actually achieved it in a few places. But the movement toward equality was fitful, as temporary victories were followed by periods of reaction.

In their desire to live richer lives, Jews had begun participating in capitalist enterprises, adopting modern languages, and contributing notably to the cultural life of their countries. While some accepted baptism as a way of accelerating assimilation and personal advancement, most maintained their allegiance to Judaism in its traditional or modified forms. Politically, they became active and visible on the left, allying themselves with the liberals, democrats, and socialists who sought a life of dignity for all men. Their economic, religious, and political choices, however, helped to awaken a broad front of opposition to Jewish emancipation.

Churchmen, who took the inferiority of Judaism as an article of faith, argued that granting Jews political rights would weaken "the Christian state." Artisans and merchants, opposed to occupational freedom for Jews, petitioned and rioted, claiming unfair competition and dishonest business practices. Conservatives, frightened by the dismantling of traditional values and hierarchies, pictured Jews as inherently destructive agents of social decomposition. Even in the camp of sympathetic allies, individuals occasionally questioned whether Jews were deserving of equal rights. Socialists attacked "parasitical" Jewish bankers as the epitome of bourgeois society's shortcomings. Liberals doubted their national loyalties. Democrats denounced Orthodox Judaism for clinging to superstition and empty ritual.

Opponents of emancipation customarily spoke in the name of high-minded principle, reluctant to admit that they were also defending special interests against the threat posed by unfettered Jewish competition. Consciously or not, all of them appealed to inherited prejudice to strengthen their own positions against what they perceived as "the Jewish danger." In virtually a reflex reaction, they stigmatized new cultural trends, objectionable political movements, threatening economic developments, or rival interests as "Jewish." Jewish participation in any of these areas constituted, in itself, an argument against them. The argument was persuasive because society at large was still riddled with anti-Jewish feeling. There was a "Jewish question" because Jews, despite acculturation and attempted assimilation, still appeared to most Europeans as essentially alien.

In Central Europe, where antisemitic ideology was born, legal equality came in the 1860s as a gift of government, not by acclamation of the people, who continued to regard Jews with deep suspicion. Using their new freedom, Jews as a group prospered as never before, entering universities, the professions, and branches of the economy from which they had previously been excluded. They became prominent in liberal and socialist politics and even gained places of authority in state administrations. Given the negative general feelings about them, their upward social mobility was bound to awaken discontent. The economic crash of 1873 and the ensuing depression rendered that discontent politically dangerous.

Antisemites were quick to relate the prosperity of Jews to their emancipation. Emancipation, they argued, signaled a critical reversal in the relations between Jews and non-Jews. It granted not mere equality but also the power to dominate. This hostile response to the new freedom included a body of traditional ideas about Jews and programs of action to deal with "the Jewish problem." Antisemitism thus entered the political cultures of many lands and a great variety of social milieus. For many, blaming Jews for social, economic, and cultural problems had become a legitimate political point of view by the end of the nineteenth century.

The *Protocols of the Elders of Zion* exploited the already quite familiar strategies of antisemitic politics: guilt by association; outlandish and unprovable charges; appeals to fear, envy, and hatred; scapegoating; and demonization. But the use of these established techniques does not wholly explain the phenomenal popularity of the *Protocols* or how it became the most widely circulated antisemitic work in history. This success is attributable at least in part to the book's literary qualities and its innovations.

By the turn of the century, the diatribes typical of antisemitic polemics seemed to be preaching only to the converted. To reach the broader public that was hostile toward Jews yet suspicious of antisemitic motives, a new device was needed. The forgers of the *Protocols* cleverly answered this need. By pretending the book was of Jewish authorship, an "authentic" document that had luckily fallen into the hands of the intended victims of Jewish plotting, the authors skirted the issue of their own motives and relieved themselves of the necessity of proving their horrific charges. The *Protocols* appeared to the public to be the unguarded revelation of the secret leaders of Jewry, the terrifying blueprint for world conquest, and the uncanny fulfillment of ancient prophecies. It was to be the wake-up call that would finally persuade apathetic readers of the Jewish peril.

Another characteristic of the piece, in this case accidental, made it especially well-suited for worldwide distribution. The work of many hands, drawing upon many sources, the *Protocols* was truly a European creation. The component parts of the myth of a Jewish-Masonic world conspiracy were contributed by a French political satirist, several priests, and a German petty bureaucrat turned novelist; Russian policemen fashioned the document, and a religious mystic prepared it for publication. The *Protocols* was written in French, translated into Russian, then translated back into French and into German, English, Swedish, Danish, Norwegian, Finnish, Romanian, Hungarian, Lithuanian, Polish, Bulgarian, Italian, and Greek. A Spanish-language edition prepared by a German publisher in 1930 carried an introduction by a Frenchman and was earmarked for distribution in South America. Dissemination of the book fell to many whose nationalities and occupations are no longer ascertainable.

Unlike almost every other antisemitic work, the book has no national context or identity. It names few names, speaks to no specifically national problem, and is therefore able to serve a great variety of purposes. Its many publishers, annotators, commentators, and translators, unimpeded by scruple, did what amounted to filling in the blanks to make the work appear appropriate to the targeted audience. Thus, in Germany the Jewish world conspiracy worked hand in glove with the victorious Allies of World War I, while in Great Britain the Germans appeared as the accomplices of the Jews. In America, Jews, said to be in cahoots with the English, were declared the real winners of the world war. Over its long career, the *Protocols of the Elders of Zion* has proved infinitely adaptable.

Finally, the style of the *Protocols* is particularly apt. It speaks the language of what the Germans call the "revolver press," the scandalmongering newspapers that form the staple reading matter for the recently literate of every country. Sensational revelations, tawdry exposés of corruption in high places, and chilling stories of degeneracy titillate readers and simultaneously convince them of their own moral superiority. This is the authentic voice of the *Protocols*.

Clearly, the book addresses an audience not thought capable of sustained reasoning. Repetitious and devoid of an organizing principle, long-winded, and stylistically barren, the *Protocols* hammers again and again at what the Jewish conspiracy entails: a hypocritical championing of democratic ideas and institutions; the supplanting of reigning governments; and the form and features of the new supergovernment to be established after the imminent conquest of the world. The conspiracy described is incredibly convoluted, but these basic aims come across forcefully indeed.

§

Binjamin W. Segel, like most others who took the field against the *Protocols of the Elders of Zion*, was not a famous or powerful man. His early recognition of the work's inherent dangers and his courage in speaking out against them are what distinguish him from more illustrious contemporaries who remained silent or oblivious. Although the author's personality, humane values, and seriousness of purpose, as well as his wit and anger, emerge clearly in his essay, the biographical details of his life are scanty.

Segel was born in 1866 in a small town in Galicia, then a part of the Austrian Empire inhabited by Poles, Ukrainians, and Jews. Like many Jews of his generation, he identified with "superior" German culture, choosing to speak, write, and think in the German language. He studied natural science, philosophy, and history at the University of Lemberg (Lwow) and then at the University of Berlin. He lived in Vienna and in Berlin, but he did not become a citizen of Germany. Whether this was by choice or the result of difficulties thrown in the way of full citizenship for *Ostjuden* (Eastern European Jews) is not known.

Although he published several short stories and one play, *Der Wald* (The forest; 1914), an expression of his abiding interest in folklore, Segel was essentially a professional journalist. According to colleagues, he was easy-going but hard-working, so that in addition to hundreds of signed and unsigned articles for various journals, he still found time to write longer books, including an early study of Bolshevism, the Jewish question in Romania and Poland, and the effects of World War I on the Jews of Eastern Europe.[3] He was regarded as an expert on Zionism although he was not an adherent of the movement. He died in 1931 after a long illness, before his worst fears concerning the *Protocols* could become reality under the Nazis.

His popular exposé of the *Protocols of the Elders of Zion* reads like an engrossing detective story. Segel gathers the evidence, uncovers original sources, compares variants to prove plagiarism, and demolishes the specious arguments of the forgery's many publishers. Building his case on the text's flagrant inner contradictions, he quashes with scathing irony all claims of authenticity made on behalf of the *Protocols*. For those with open minds, his book still performs an essential service.

Segel's analysis of the myth of Jewish world conspiracy, notably its historical origins and the development of its component parts, is a tribute to his powers of textual criticism. He exercises the same care and thoroughness when discussing the national contexts into which the *Protocols* was injected. But having only limited access to the sources that might have better explained the motives and political forces behind the success of the *Protocols,* Segel sometimes goes beyond what the evidence will support. Much has been learned since he wrote his critique in the mid-1920s, and some of his interpretation now requires revision.

Segel's account of the origin of the *Protocols of the Elders of Zion* has become part of the general scholarly consensus. Between its fabrication in Paris in 1897–98 and the revolutionary events in Russia of 1905, the as yet unpublished *Protocols* appears to have had no purpose beyond influencing the policies and rather minor personnel decisions of Tsar Nicholas II. Segel, along with most other scholars, sees the 1905 Russian publication of the *Protocols* in book form as a sinister escalation of the forgery's functions. To preempt forces working for change, a shadowy collection of secret policemen, reactionary aristocrats, extreme nationalists, and religious cranks sought to discredit liberal reformers by associating them with Jews and by representing the tsar's reform-minded ministers as the dupes or agents of Jews. Read properly, the *Protocols* urged upon the tsar and the supporters of his autocracy the necessity for ruthless repression of its enemies.

In considering the actual, as opposed to the intended, influence of the *Protocols of the Elders of Zion* on tsarist policy, Segel is cautious but does not wholly escape the common view of his day that the *Protocols* swiftly became the official policy of tsarism, a freely wielded weapon designed to turn the masses loose on defenseless Jews. Furthermore, the mounting influence of the *Protocols* was inconceivable without the active and passive collusion of high-ranking ministers of state. Segel relies on circumstantial evidence to argue this case. He concluded, as did many of his contemporaries (and ours), that the government of Russia used the *Protocols* as antisemitic propaganda and the resulting antisemitic violence as a conscious instrument of power. How valid is this contention?

Ever since the partitions of Poland at the end of the eighteenth century placed half the world's Jews under the rule of the tsars, more or less rigorous forms of official persecution prevailed. As in central and western Europe, the roots of Jew-hatred in Russia went back to ancient religious conflicts. In addition, the middleman economic functions performed by Jews rendered them loathsome to a largely peasant society. Russian literature, with few exceptions, portrayed them negatively. From the late 1860s, political commentators on both left and right also attacked them in print. But as opposition to a retrograde autocracy grew in the 1870s, a section of the intelligentsia underwent a change of heart. Progressives began to see the tsar's oppression of Jews as a shabby stratagem to deflect attention from his own shortcomings; they responded by backing Jewish emancipation.

When the first great mob actions against Jews took place in the wake of the assassination of Tsar Alexander II in 1881, many within and outside Russia believed that the government had orchestrated the violence. In the following decades, the regime tolerated, and even sponsored, antisemitic organizations and propaganda, allowing censors to pass antisemitic books and articles. While elsewhere European governments, democratic and authoritarian, were doing away with Jewish legal disabilities, the tsars maintained them virtually intact.

The Russia of Alexander III (1881–94) and Nicholas II (1894–1917) pursued legal and administrative policies that were antisemitic. But did the government actually foment and organize anti-Jewish violence? Little hard evidence exists to support this contention. After the anti-Jewish riots of 1881, in which high-level officials may have had a hand, the central government consistently resisted a repetition, dismissing the authorities who had not acted promptly to quell the violence and punishing the perpetrators. Moreover, the government maintained that its anti-Jewish policies actually reflected the will of the people and that such measures, in fact, prevented worse from happening. This line of reasoning held that if Jews were emancipated, the people's full fury would be turned against both the Jews and the government. Disingenuous though it sounds, this argument may have seemed valid for those in power. No doubt official Russia had little regard for the well-being of Jews, but the stirring up of mob violence was too dangerous a tactic for an autocracy increasingly unsure of its popular support. Rulers lacked the confidence that they could safely manipulate the emotions of the people for a controlled end. Violence against defenseless Jews could too easily be turned against government itself.

If, as Segel suspected, high government officials lurked behind the fabrication of the *Protocols of the Elders of Zion,* they took no steps to use it as popular propaganda to stir up the masses. Although passed by the police censors, the book was classified as ineligible for mass distribution. Consequently, the *Protocols* never reached a mass audience in tsarist Russia and therefore never realized its full political potential. The book failed even in the narrower goal of swaying the antisemitic Nicholas II. In 1906, after receiving a copy of the book from one of his officials, he forbade its further dissemination: "It is impossible," he reportedly said, "to defend something sacred [Imperial Russia] by dirty methods."[4]

Taking these qualifications into consideration, Segel's conclusion needs modification. The tsarist government may have used antisemitism for its own purposes and certainly did little or nothing to combat anti-Jewish hostility in the general public. It is unlikely, however, that government was directly responsible for the spread of violence against Jews after the 1880s. With regard to the *Protocols,* there is no convincing evidence that the central authorities used the book as an instrument of power. The supporters of tsarism outside government were responsible for keeping the book alive, but they apparently acted without extensive help from official circles.[5]

Without the Russian Revolution of 1917, the *Protocols of the Elders of Zion* might have remained the obsession of reactionary imaginations, unknown to the world at large. The book certainly would never have achieved any serious political importance. However, the revolution, the civil war, and the international communist movement gave birth to a powerful new myth. "Judeo-Bolshevism" rescued the *Protocols* from obscurity and has proved the most effective basis for its spread and its credibility. To the supporters of Russian autocracy who fled west with the *Protocols* in their baggage, the Bolshevik Revolution was the unmistakable work of a Jewish conspiracy. And they found in Europe, North and South America, and the Muslim world a large audience prepared to believe that this was so. Responsible lay and spiritual leaders, politicians, and respected newspaper publishers — people who should have known better — were too easily persuaded that events in Russia constituted a Jewish assault on Western civilization itself.

Seeing Bolshevism as "Jewish" relies on a deliberately selective reading of facts and a predisposition to see Jews as the agents of evil. When, in October 1905, Nicholas II averred that 90 percent of all revolutionaries were Jews, it was his way of denying that true Russians were rebelling against him. It was true that Jews were to be found in the ranks of every anti-tsarist and reform movement. But in this they behaved no differently than many other persecuted minorities of the Russian Empire. Desperate self-defense, especially since their experience of violence and discrimination in the 1880s, rather than "revenge against Christian civilization" dictated this oppositional course of action for Jews. What should have been seen as a legitimate response to oppression instead fed existing suspicions about Jewish plotting.

Nor do the statistics of Jewish participation in anti-tsarist movements make a persuasive case for "Judeo-Bolshevism." As elsewhere in Europe wherever liberalism existed as an option, the great majority of Jews preferred it over more extreme political tendencies. In prerevolutionary Russia, the Kadets, a liberal, middle-class reform group, drew the most Jewish support. Poorer Jews and the Jewish intelligentsia, however, saw socialism as the solution to both tsarist autocracy and the class conflict that raged in their communities. Jews were highly visible in the leadership of the peasant-populist Social Revolutionary Party. The General Jewish Workers' Bund, founded in 1897, attracted the Jewish proletariat and reached a membership of thirty-four thousand by 1917. In the small Menshevik faction of the Russian Social Democratic Party, Jews were numerous and prominent. On the other hand, Lenin's Bolshevik faction of the RSPD counted fewer Jews as members than any of its anti-tsarist competitors. According to the party census of 1922, approximately one thousand Jews, or 4 percent of the membership, joined the Bolsheviks before 1917 and another twelve hundred in that revolutionary year.

These numbers apply only to the politically active, a quite small percentage of the entire Jewish population of Imperial Russia. For the politically passive and traditionally observant majority, Bolshevism had little to offer. The religiously orthodox spurned atheistic Marxism. Zionists and Bundists rejected the Bolsheviks' denial of Jewish nationality. Although the Jews of Russia were far from prosperous, they were nonetheless largely middle- or lower-middle-class businessmen, artisans, or workers in small factories. Most had every reason to fear the consequences if a party of the industrial proletariat won power.

Yet, statistics aside, individual Jews certainly played a prominent role in Lenin's movement. Leon Trotsky created the Red Army. Grigori Zinoviev led the Communist International (Comintern). Lev Kamenev, along with Trotsky and Zinoviev, sat on the Politburo. And even before Lenin attempted to extend the Russian Revolution throughout the world, Jews had taken leadership roles in what became the Communist parties of Hungary, Germany, and Poland. They also held pivotal positions in secondary levels of party leadership in both the Soviet Union and elsewhere. Because they were literate and rootless — that is, without close bonds to the larger national societies in which the Communists operated — Jews frequently held key posts in the secret police and in the propaganda and economic planning agencies. Thus, by pointing to the Jewish names among the party functionaries, antisemites and anticommunists won easy converts to the notion of Judeo-Bolshevism in the general population of countries affected or threatened by Communism.

It was perhaps asking too much of fearful people that they distinguish between activists of Jewish descent and the Jews as a group. But the differences were important. Like Karl Marx and several others instrumental in the revolutionary labor movement, the Jews who joined the Communist parties had severed all connections to Jewish religion and culture. They were secularists whose identity and values were formed by the movement and whose Jewish roots were often an embarrassment, even in a party that pretended to be indifferent to ethnicity. Jews joined communist movements for a variety of reasons. Some were idealists, seeking social justice and a world without war and bigotry. Others were rank opportunists, careerists, or adventurers.

These differences were immaterial to many horrified observers for whom the Bolshevik Revolution was an unalloyed nightmare, explainable only as the work of nihilists and criminals. Such a description fit the preexisting Jewish stereotype too closely to be resisted. Jews as a group, as a "race," according to antisemitic ideology, were intrinsically Bolshevik, instinctively destructive, no matter the outward, superficial differences among them. Reverting to form, the Christ-killing, well-poisoning, internationally connected Jew had once again unleashed a new affliction upon humanity.

But despite the assertion that communism was the tool of the Jews, few Jews actually prospered under its rule. Even the Bolshevik elite of Jewish descent did not fare well. During the purge trials of the 1930s, Stalin arranged for the judicial murder of his major competitors and former comrades, Kamenev and Zinoviev, along with many other Jewish functionaries. He had Trotsky assassinated in Mexico City in 1940 and used and then liquidated several Jews in the Sovietization of Eastern Europe after World War II.

When Jews managed to improve their social and economic situation in the USSR, finally rising above the obstacles tsarism had placed in their way, the price was high in terms of Jewish identity. After the revolution, Lenin pursued a policy designed to weaken Judaism and eradicate antisemitism; he succeeded only with the former aim. Outside the Soviet Union, wherever communists exercised power after 1917, and especially after 1945, they acted with particular harshness against Jews, expropriating or deporting them as the "bourgeois class enemy." Jewish religious and cultural institutions and competing political movements received no better treatment than the non-Jewish. In the implementation of their program, Jewish and non-Jewish communists were utterly "objective" and indistinguishable from one another.

However, the perception of reality, not reality itself, is often what counts in politics. In a good part of the world after World War I, the myth of Judeo-Bolshevism enjoyed wide currency, counterevidence notwithstanding. The massive dislocations of war and revolution made it possible for the *Protocols of the Elders of Zion* to become a force in politics. Among all the countries in crisis, none was as well disposed to accept the "truth" of the *Protocols* as Germany.

§

Binjamin Segel wrote for a German audience. He was prompted by his anxiety about the effect of the *Protocols* on political life in his adopted country. Like most cultured Europeans of his era, he viewed Russia as a barbaric land, a place "where anything could happen." That religious zealots and secret policemen should produce a forged document for reactionary political purposes simply confirmed his preconceptions. On the other hand, that the same document should be taken seriously in a civilized place like Germany, the "land of poets and thinkers," he found both surprising and disturbing.

Segel had reason to be disturbed—but not surprised. German vulnerability to the *Protocols* had been prepared well before several anti-Bolshevik White Russians began circulating the document in 1918. For forty years, the German antisemitic political parties had inundated Protestant peasants and lower-middle-class town dwellers, both economically beset groups, with antisemitic slogans and literature. Other parties, at times, also employed such tactics. In 1892, the aristocratic Conservative Party sought votes from this same constituency by writing an antisemitic plank into its national program. Its agrarian lobbying agency was instrumental in the spread of racist-nationalist antisemitism before and during World War I. National Liberals and the Catholic Center Party occasionally violated their own principles with antisemitic electioneering. Only the left-liberal and Social Democratic parties refrained from this sort of campaigning.

Although the specifically antisemitic political parties never won much support in prewar German politics, they and the opportunistic Conservatives were not alone in demanding a solution to the Jewish question. A number of occupational associations, cultural societies, and nationalist groups also swelled the stream of antisemitic discourse. The Pan-German League, an organization with an elite middle-class membership, produced its own racist–nationalist literature independent of party politics. Leading figures in German public life, such as the chaplain to the royal court, Adolf Stoecker, the very popular historian Heinrich von Treitschke, and the world-famous composer Richard Wagner, vented their hostility toward Jews and helped legitimize the public expression of these attitudes.

The notion that Jews were engaged in a conspiracy of worldwide dimensions predated by many decades the appearance of the *Protocols of the Elders of Zion*. At the birth of antisemitic politics, Wilhelm Marr had described the Jews' "eighteen hundred year war" against Germany and the world as a racial conspiracy in his best-selling *Victory of Jewry over Germandom* (1879). A generation later, Theodor Fritsch, a tireless publisher of antisemitic literature, anticipated the *Protocols* when he explained the "unleashing" of the world war, still in its early stages, as the secret work of Freemasons and Jews, the real rulers of world politics.

While full-time antisemitic ideologues and politicians like Marr and Fritsch had an audience before and during the war, they and their lower-middle-class colleagues were not major forces in political life before 1918. Not many Germans could be fairly described as committed antisemites, absolutely convinced that the Jewish question was of life-and-death importance to national survival, and therefore prepared to take action. At most, agitators and publicists made the public discussion of Jewish evil a familiar and acceptable topic in German-speaking Europe. Thanks to their efforts, age-old suspicions of Jews were kept alive, and large parts of the public continued to distrust and dislike them.

Postwar events worsened this situation. Crisis after crisis destabilized Germany, making possible the kind of antisemitic extremism that provided the ideal growing medium for the *Protocols of the Elders of Zion.* The disastrous war and revolution, the collapse of a five-hundred-year-old dynasty, the harsh peace settlement, coups from the right and the left, political assassinations, and hyperinflation had devastating consequences for Germany's first experiment in democracy, the Weimar Republic. Born in defeat, and the intellectual product of liberals and socialists, many of them Jewish, the republic became the target of nationalist, conservative, and radical rightist hatred. An antisemitic interpretation of the German collapse and world disorder, such as the *Protocols* provided, had much to recommend it to these political tendencies.

Segel identifies two sets of motives at work in the propagation of the *Protocols* in Germany. For the antisemitic activists in numerous lower-middle-class parties, organizations, and paramilitary groups, the book confirmed everything they had always believed. Authenticity was not an issue. For years the activists had warned an apathetic country about the exponential growth of Jewish power. The *Protocols* was a godsend, the document that would finally convince their countrymen to recognize the Jewish danger and to take action.

The sponsorship of the *Protocols* by upper-class Germans like Otto zu Salm, mentioned by Segel, was founded on a different rationale, one more cynical and desperate, similar to the original aims of the document in tsarist Russia. Quite perceptively, Segel recognized that disseminating the *Protocols* served the political interests of large groups of important Germans, that the enterprise did not depend simply on the foibles or moral failings of prominent individuals.

The German elite of property and education — aristocrats, industrialists, army officers, professors, and high-ranking civil servants — had ruled the kaiser's Germany but faced an uncertain future in a democracy. The German Revolution of 1918 and the diffident leaders of the Weimar Republic left many of these people in place, although no longer all-powerful. With the specter of the Russian Revolution before their eyes, they feared the worst. A "Bolshevik Germany" might dispossess them as completely as their Russian counterparts.

Prince Salm, General Erich Ludendorff (also mentioned by

Segel), and several others from among the former ruling elite leapt at the opportunity presented by the *Protocols*. Privately, several of these individuals expressed doubts about the genuineness of the document, but they nonetheless recognized how it could enable them to escape responsibility for a disastrous war and to undermine the dreaded Weimar Republic. Jews were already deeply unpopular in broad sectors of German society, and the miseries attendant on defeat only intensified anti-Jewish feeling. The *Protocols* blamed Jews for starting the war, showed how revolution was one of their stock weapons, and claimed that the democratic republic was the conspirators' preferred means of conquest. To those about to be pushed from power by defeat and revolution, all these accusations fit Germany's situation or could be made to fit it after slight "editing" of the Russian edition of the *Protocols*. If the "mob," held in utter contempt by its social betters, could be made to believe this rendition of history, perhaps the prestige and power of former days could be salvaged. At the very least, the progress of democracy could be slowed.

One of the factors that had kept the antisemitic political movement from assuming greater importance in prewar Germany had been its inability to secure steady support from the socially and economically powerful. In the closing days of the war, this gap was bridged by the Pan-German League, whose members had lofty social credentials and connections. Finally convinced that Germany had lost the military contest, the league declared all-out war against Jewry in October 1918. Jews, its vice-president said, would be made to serve as the "lightning rod for all the discontent of the masses." The league provided funds for the German translation of the *Protocols* published by Gottfried zur Beek and, just as important, helped to found the Deutschvölkisch Schutz- und Trutzbund (German National Association for Offense and Defense), an umbrella organization that united several rightist groups. The association, which grew to nearly eight hundred thousand members before being banned in 1923, had a conspiratorial wing that engaged in violence against political enemies and a public branch that saw to the marketing of the *Protocols*. In the chaos of postwar Germany, funding and fanaticism came together, allowing the *Protocols* to achieve swiftly the political influence that had eluded it in tsarist Russia.

§

Parallel to the developments in Germany, the *Protocols of the Elders of Zion* also struck deep roots in the United States. Here, too, anti-Bolshevik Russian refugees introduced typescripts of the document to cabinet, judiciary, and military intelligence officials. Then, in a stroke of fortune, it made its way to the industrialist Henry Ford, whose backing secured a permanent place in American life for the *Protocols*.

Americans were by no means prepared to take the *Protocols* as seriously as Germans. The United States had emerged from the world war stable, virtually unscathed, and the creditor to other nations. Yet antisemitism was not unknown here. The Europeans who settled America brought with them historical anti-Jewish prejudices. During the colonial era Jews could not vote or hold public office. They met unequal treatment in law courts and were sometimes subject to occupational restrictions. Individual states, unhindered by the federal Constitution, were able legally to discriminate against Jews in appointments to public office.

In the United States, too, Jews were grossly caricatured and reviled in pamphlets, newspapers, and both high and low literature. From the 1870s, fashionable hotels and resorts often refused Jewish guests, and residential neighborhoods were closed to Jews by so-called gentlemen's agreements. Prep schools and many universities, the most prestigious leading the way, instituted the *numerus clausus,* a percentage quota for Jewish admissions, which in some cases remained in force into the 1960s. In the 1920s, employment agencies and want ads in newspapers frequently warned, "No Jews need apply." Professional organizations and social clubs practiced a formal or a casual brand of exclusion. Even more disturbing, mob violence occasionally claimed a Jewish victim, as in 1915 when Leo Frank was lynched in Atlanta after being wrongfully accused of killing a Christian girl.

American Jews appeared "different" to many of their neighbors, too powerful, too smart, too rich. They were, in fact, more middle class, more urbanized, and less likely to earn their livings by manual labor. Their supposed overrepresentation in the professions and the media, a factor that had fueled an antisemitic political response in Germany, Austria, Hungary, Poland, and France, might well have led to the same result in the United States. But even if these preconditions for antisemitic politics existed in the United States, they were rarely exploited successfully—although not for want of trying. One of the most threatening endeavors to capitalize on native anti-Jewish prejudices and derive political advantage from them is associated with Henry Ford's advocacy of the *Protocols of the Elders of Zion*.

On 22 May 1920 Ford's recently acquired newspaper, the weekly *Dearborn Independent*, featured an unsigned lead article entitled "The International Jew, the World's Problem." Feeding off the Red scare that seized the United States after the war, the article repeated what was by then a widely accepted truth: the Jews were behind the Bolshevik Revolution, an important step in their secret government's plan of world conquest. For ninety-one successive weeks, the newspaper featured articles on the universally corrupting influence of Jewry upon American life—from jazz, short skirts, and bobbed hair to the total control of finance and the press. Starting in July 1920, the *Protocols of the Elders of Zion* came under detailed, sympathetic discussion for several weeks. Subsequently, the collected articles appeared as a four-volume book, *The International Jew*.

Unlike the surreptitious funders of the *Protocols* in Germany, Ford openly threw his reputation and his resources, both enormous, behind a major ad campaign. The *Dearborn Independent* preached traditional values of sobriety, hard work, and thrift to its largely rural readership; the paper reached a circulation of approximately three hundred thousand and sold for five cents a copy or one dollar a year. *The International Jew*, eventually translated into sixteen languages, cost twenty-five cents per volume. Five hundred thousand copies were in circulation in the United States alone. Still, by 1928 Ford had lost nearly five million dollars in these publishing ventures. Evidently, profit was not his motive.

Ford's reasons for disseminating the *Protocols* and for attempting to politicize anti-Jewish feeling in America remain matters of conjecture. Some have theorized that he adopted antisemitism to serve his presidential ambitions or that he was responding to setbacks in other grand political and economic schemes. Others have seen his antisemitism as long-standing and personal, the result of his exposure as a farm boy to American populism, a movement that blamed eastern bankers and middlemen for the woes of farmers. Although hugely rich and successful, Ford was not a sophisticated man or thinker. Popularly revered as the Great Simplifier, he had a genius for finding shortcut solutions to problems of industrial production. It is not surprising, therefore, that antisemitism, which proffered the simplest solutions to the thorniest problems of modern life, should appeal to such a man.[6]

The American career of the *Protocols* demonstrated the forgery's versatility once again. The articles in the *Dearborn Independent* were written by professional journalists, whose tone differed markedly from European treatments of the *Protocols*. Matter-of-fact and not overtly fanatical, with a pretense of discussing the pros and cons of the issues, the articles nevertheless left little doubt as to the reality of the Jewish world conspiracy. Topics such as Freemasonry, which was far less suspect in the United States than in Europe, or autocracy and aristocracy, which had no relevance to an American audience, were largely ignored in Ford's newspaper and book and in the dozens of new versions of the *Protocols* that have appeared here from the 1920s to the 1990s. Instead, the emphasis is on the Jewish danger to public morality, the corruption of Christian youth, and, of course, Judeo-Bolshevism.

Ford recanted his views publicly in 1927, stopped publication of *The International Jew,* and apologized for any harm he might have done. But it is fairly certain that this was no more than a diplomatic retreat, taken when he was about to lose a libel suit. After his disavowal, the *Protocols* found a home among fundamentalist Christian and right-wing anticommunist organizations. Since 1920, more than one hundred editions, reprintings, and new versions of the *Protocols* and *The International Jew* have appeared in the English-speaking world, most of them in the United States. Except briefly during the Great Depression of the 1930s, the diatribes have remained of minimal political importance.[7]

The harm Ford did was nevertheless considerable. His prestige helped make antisemitic attacks respectable in America and elsewhere. To antisemites looking for credibility, the name Henry Ford proved useful indeed. Among his sincerest admirers was Adolf Hitler, who kept a photograph of the "heroic American, Heinrich Ford."[8] Ford's *The International Jew* continued to appear in Germany well after he asked that it be withdrawn. Theodor Fritsch, for example, refused to believe that the request was sincere, claiming that it was yet more proof of the Jewish conspiracy: Jewry's money power could bring even the American millionaire to his knees.

§

Even as interest in the *Protocols* seemed to have peaked in the United States, the forgery was gathering new strength in Germany. There as nowhere else the myth of Jewish world conspiracy intruded into mainstream politics. Prestigious newspapers discussed the *Protocols*; political terrorists invoked it as the rationale for their acts; and many groups on the far right used it to focus anger against Jews and the Weimar Republic. Among the rightists, Hitler and the Nazi Party did not appear especially significant in the mid-1920s; Segel does not even mention them by name. The fiasco of the beerhall putsch in 1923 and Hitler's subsequent imprisonment led many contemporaries to write off the rowdy, largely Bavarian enterprise. Segel was not alone in failing to take the Nazis seriously. However, the later career of the *Protocols of the Elders of Zion* is unintelligible without them.

Individual Nazis took an early interest in the book. Baldur von Schirach, eventual leader of the Hitler Youth, said he was converted to antisemitism at age seventeen after reading Ford's *The International Jew*. Alfred Rosenberg, the "official" philosopher of the party and a Baltic German refugee, may have been one of the intermediaries between White Russian carriers of the *Protocols* and its German publishers. In 1923 Rosenberg published his own extensive commentary on the *Protocols* and reprinted it three times before the year was out. In 1929 the Nazi Party bought the rights to zur Beek's original edition of 1920, reprinting a shorter version twenty-two times by 1938. When the Nazis took power in 1933, perhaps one hundred thousand copies of the numerous variants of the *Protocols,* along with several thousand abridgments of Ford's *The International Jew,* were circulating within Germany. Books about or based upon the *Protocols* made its message generally available.

What Adolf Hitler thought of and learned from the *Protocols of the Elders of Zion* is, like so many other aspects of his worldview, a matter of some debate. There is no doubt, however, that the question has significance, for on Hitler's ideological authority the Nazi state undertook the murder of millions of Jews. Did Hitler's belief in the *Protocols* move him to genocide?

In *Mein Kampf* (1925–26), Hitler said he became an antisemite in his Vienna years (1907–13) on the basis of first-hand observation and personal suffering. Before leaving Vienna for Munich, he had ample opportunity to learn from the most successful prewar antisemitic politician, Mayor Karl Lueger (1844–1910). After serving in World War I, Hitler returned to Munich, working for the army as a nationalist propagandist among demobilizing troops. Sent by his superiors to evaluate the German Workers' Party, shortly to become the National Socialist Workers' Party, he instead became a member and soon left the army to devote himself exclusively to politics. He joined his shrill voice to those already decrying the financial power of Jewry, attributing the world war and its loss to "international Jewish capitalists," condemning the government that protected these criminals and demanding that they be hanged.

Hitler, aside from the crudity of his language concerning the Jews, appeared to be just another of the lower-middle-class agitators and conventional antisemites who had been active on the fringes of German politics even before the war. But in the feverish competition for public attention, he quickly distinguished himself by the radicalism of his positions and the violence of his rhetoric. In Munich he came in contact with several racist–nationalist thinkers, among them Rosenberg. Under their tutelage, his view of the Jewish danger expanded greatly. His mentors informed him of the Jewishness of the Bolshevik Revolution and educated him to the full dimensions of the Jewish world conspiracy. Eventually, the elimination of Jewish Bolshevism and the acquisition of living space in the Soviet sphere became the unifying element in his worldview, leading to World War II and the Holocaust.

It is likely that the *Protocols of the Elders of Zion* played a role in the transformation of Hitler's antisemitism. Whether he read the book himself and was immediately convinced of its truth, as he claimed, or was influenced by others who had read it is not an answerable question, perhaps not even an important one. The "logic" of the *Protocols* was all-pervasive on the German right, even among those who had never read the book. At the very least, the *Protocols* corroborated what Hitler had come to believe about the nature of Jewish evil. His first mention of the work, in August 1921, came in a speech devoted to the mounting German inflation. Inflation, he said, repeating the wisdom of the *Protocols,* was just another word for hunger — part of the Jews' strategy to undermine nations scheduled for conquest. It was also an intentional product of the Treaty of Versailles, which itself was the work of the Jews' stooge, Woodrow Wilson, his 117 Jewish bankers, and the Anglo-French Jews.[9] Apparently, Hitler had made the cosmic and all-embracing explanation of world events found in the *Protocols* his own.

Some have argued that it was not only Hitler's worldview that registered the influence of the *Protocols.* He may actually have acquired power and governed his empire by following the recipes of the Elders of Zion. One of his confidants, a Nazi who later turned against the movement, reported this conversation:

"In those [early] days [of our movement] I read the *Protocols of the Elders of Zion* — I was really shocked," [said Hitler]. "The perilous stealth of the enemy, and his omnipresence! I saw at once that we would have to imitate this — in our own way, of course. . . . "

"Don't you think," I objected, "that you are overestimating the Jews?"

"No, no, no!" Hitler screamed. "It is not possible to exaggerate the Jew as an enemy."

"But," I said, "the *Protocols* are an obvious forgery. I learned about them in 1920 from a certain Müller von Hausen [Gottfried zur Beek]. And it was immediately evident to me that they could not possibly be genuine."

"Why not?" Hitler said, getting angry. Whether they were genuine in an historical sense was not the issue for him. Their inner truth was what made them so convincing.

"We must strike at the Jews with their own weapons. That was clear to me as soon as I read the book."

I asked, "Were you inspired by the *Protocols* in your [political] struggle?"

"Yes, indeed, and in detail. I learned enormously from these *Protocols*."[10]

Hitler's political techniques certainly bore more similarity to the mythical Elders than anything real Jews have done or have been in a position to do. But the quoted conversation does not prove that Hitler learned his methods by studying the *Protocols*. He did not need to be instructed in the use of political intrigue, conspiracy, revolutionary disruption, camouflage, and diversion. These techniques of modern dictators or would-be dictators do not require literary inspiration.

Whatever Hitler learned from or thought about the *Protocols,* his regime adopted the forgery as part of its official ideology and became the book's most active propagator from 1933 on. Distillations of the text appeared in the classroom, indoctrinated the Hitler Youth, and invaded the USSR along with German soldiers. German propaganda agencies distributed the book to Latin America and financed publication in several other European countries. Their efforts were not always welcome and in two cases produced a legal counterattack.

In South Africa and Switzerland the *Protocols* went on trial. "A fraud and a hoax" was the verdict in both proceedings. Forced to prove their fantasies in courts of law, the champions of the forgery found it indefensible. Expert witnesses from several countries, relying on Segel's study significantly in their testimony, shredded all claims of authenticity. The judge in the Swiss trial concluded the proceedings, leaving no doubt as to his feelings: "I hope that there will come a time when nobody will any longer understand how in the year 1935 almost a dozen fully sane and reasonable men could for fourteen days torment their brains before a court at Bern over the authenticity or lack of authenticity of these so-called "protocols," these *Protocols* that, despite all the harm they have caused and may yet cause, are nothing but ridiculous nonsense."[11]

Measuring the harm done by the *Protocols of the Elders of Zion* admits of no exactitude. We cannot know what those who read the book thought about the myth or how exposure to it affected their behavior. Claims are often heard that the *Protocols* directly inspired violence against Jews in Kishinev (1903) and Buenos Aires (1919) or that it bore major responsibility in the deaths of 120,000 Jews during the Russian civil war, as Segel asserts. But the *Protocols* did not appear in Kishinev or Buenos Aires until after the anti-Jewish riots there.[12] It was introduced apparently to justify previous violence and, perhaps, to prepare the way for new outbreaks, which, however, failed to materialize. Although widely distributed in the Ukraine during the Russian civil war, the book was in all likelihood more of an inspiration to the leaders of the White armies than to their peasant soldiers, whose long-standing grievances against Jews needed no additional stimulus.

In modern times, the greatest violence against Jews occurred during the Holocaust. What the *Protocols* contributed to this horror is, again, not fully measurable. The foremost modern authority on the subject has suggested in the title of his book that the *Protocols* was vitally important to the Holocaust, that it served as nothing less than a "warrant for genocide."[13] Such a formulation is problematical. It tends to reduce a complex event to too simple a cause and to make the *Protocols* itself into something of a myth. For those few men who decided that mass murder ought to be the "Final Solution of the Jewish Question," the Jews' conspiratorial ambitions, as depicted in the *Protocols,* may have supplied the rationale for action. The hypothesis, although unprovable, is not unreasonable.

But what of the thousands who actively collaborated in extermination, let alone the millions who passively witnessed the increasing persecution that led up to it? Would their actions have been different had there never existed a *Protocols of the Elders of Zion*? It is apparent that the Nazis consciously used the *Protocols* to win mass support for their anti-Jewish policies. They attempted to convince Germans and the rest of the world that Jews were an enormous danger to all mankind. But the *Protocols,* although important, was only one tool that relentlessly drove this dehumanizing message home. When legal persecution became mass murder, however, the myth of Jewish world conspiracy and the mass support it was supposed to engender became less directly significant. Although the *Protocols* attributes every known evil to Jews and, at least by implication, encourages their victims to defend themselves, it does not urge mass extermination or, for that matter, any specific solution of the Jewish question. Furthermore, the perpetrators of the Final Solution needed no warrant for genocide because they were able to dispense with mass participation, making every effort to liquidate the Jews in secrecy.

The true harm of the *Protocols* lay not in its questionable capacity to stimulate direct action but rather in its encouragement of inaction. Antisemitic fanatics, ambitious national leaders, and mindlessly obedient bureaucrats initiated and administered the Final Solution. The passive acceptance of their initiatives, however, was essential. In this respect, as the most lurid description of the Jewish world conspiracy, the *Protocols* contributed to the sacrifice of the Jews. Even if ordinary people withheld their full belief in the myth, even if, like Hitler's confidant, they thought the picture of Jewish evil to be vastly exaggerated, they were suspicious enough, after decades of propaganda, to withhold their help. During the Holocaust, helping Jews escape death required enormous courage; the costs of heroism could be terrible indeed. That so few intervened had much to do with Nazi terror and cannot be wholly attributed to antisemitism. But throughout Eastern and Central Europe between the wars—that is, at a time before rendering aid became so dangerous—citizens looked on without protest, often with approval, as Jews were isolated and were deprived of civil rights, the protection of the law, and, finally, their lives. In the world at large, beyond the

reach of the Nazis, the *Protocols* helped render Jews ineligible for
rescue by the great majority of their fellowmen.

§

The Holocaust of European Jewry ought to have ended sixty-five
years of political antisemitism and the public career of the *Protocols of
the Elders of Zion*. But neither missed a beat. Counting so-called
studies of the *Protocols* and other titles that masked true contents,
there were eight fresh printings in the 1950s, sixteen in the 1960s,
twenty-three in the 1970s, twenty in the 1980s, and four thus far in
the 1990s.

The forum of the *Protocols* is all that has altered. In postwar Germany, antisemitic literature became unthinkable in the East and
illegal in the West. In the rest of Europe, however, neo-Nazis and
their sympathizers have occasionally produced new versions. In
England, the Britons Publishing Company brought out its eighty-
second impression in 1963, and in 1980 the New National Front, a
racist political party, placed the "world-famous report of a Jewish
meeting at which a blueprint was laid to control the world" on
its recommended reading list. The book has been published and
banned in Austria and Switzerland, serialized in Belgium (1967),
and republished in France (1968, 1993). A deluxe and a pocket
version appeared in Spain in 1964 and 1972. In Italy neo-Fascists
circulated the *Protocols* in 1974. Greek Orthodox circles produced
two versions in the late 1970s, and a new Polish translation came out
in 1991.

These versions of the book are clearly marginal phenomena, the
efforts of those who have forgotten nothing and learned nothing;
they have been politically unproductive. The same cannot be said of
several other situations where the *Protocols* continues to exercise its
negative influence on political life, threatening the rights and lives
of Jews. This effect was particularly apparent in Latin America and
the Soviet Union during the 1960s and 1970s. The forgery remains
influential today in the Arab world, the countries of the former
Eastern bloc, and in some quarters of the United States.

The hiatus in governmental antisemitism in the Soviet Union lasted only a short while after the revolution. Under Joseph Stalin, particularly after World War II, official policy and officially sanctioned literature revived the tradition of tsarist days. Unlike the Hitler state, the Soviet Union never defined the solution of the Jewish question as one of its tasks. It nonetheless made use of existing anti-Jewish feeling and the literature of conspiracy for political purposes.

Patriotism, rehabilitated during World War II, brought with it occasional campaigns against "internationalists" and "cosmopolitans" that served to deflect attention from Soviet economic failures and to justify the country's foreign policy. Jews, according to Leninism, were the quintessential internationalists, having no nationality or culture of their own. When Stalin died in 1953, the so-called Jewish doctors' plot against the lives of prominent officials was assuming menacing dimensions. Stalin's successors dismantled this campaign, but after the Arab-Israeli War of 1967, they launched a far more sustained effort of their own.

Because antisemitism carried the unmistakable taint of counter-revolution, a convenient fiction was contrived. "Zionists," not Jews, were the evil; it was they who engaged in a worldwide conspiracy to undermine the USSR from their headquarters in Jerusalem. To forward their global conspiratorial ambitions, "Zionists" fomented and manipulated antisemitism, sowing disunion among otherwise fraternal peoples. In fact, "Zionists" bore all the characteristics that antisemites habitually ascribed to Jews. The tenuousness of the euphemism became clear when one writer speculated that fully 90 percent of Soviet Jews were open or secret "Zionists."[14] During the 1970s the familiar depiction of world Jewry as a tightly knit, awesomely destructive force gained complete access to the state-controlled media. Between 1967 and the early 1980s, the government approved more than 150 "anti-Zionist" works, many of them clearly inspired by the *Protocols of the Elders of Zion*. In 1977, a Soviet television documentary, aired twice and commented upon extensively in the press, equated Jews with apartheid, fascism, and capitalism.

With the collapse of the Soviet Union, a more traditional and popularly based antisemitism, visible for many years in the dissident samizdat press, was suddenly free to express itself openly. Today, Jews in the former USSR once again find themselves accused of being wire-pullers, millionnaires, pornographers, warmongers, and saboteurs — criminal types that historically characterized them in the *Protocols*. The myth of Judeo-Bolshevism, which had no utility for the heirs of the revolution, is also again back in vogue. Elements of the army, press, and unions are virtually unrestrained in their antisemitic agitation. Pamyat, the most vocal of the many extremist nationalist groups, produced its own edition of the *Protocols of the Elders of Zion* in 1992.

Soviet government antisemitism helped create the climate in which the latest outbreak could take place. But government-directed antisemitism in the modern period served circumscribed ends. As a political tool, it stopped well short of overt incitement to violence. Indeed, one of its paradoxical functions was to dissuade Jews, a highly educated and skilled part of the population, from leaving the Soviet Union. The fear of being branded "Zionist," it was hoped, would pressure Jews into conformity. The latest version of antisemitism has no such purpose, and in the postcommunist crisis, with the central government no longer able to maintain absolute control, Jews appear to be in jeopardy.

The post-Holocaust career of the *Protocols* followed more traditional European lines in Latin America, arriving first in the 1920s and reappearing there in subsequent decades. Ecuador, Brazil, Mexico, Chile, Panama, and El Salvador have all seen new editions since 1945. For segments of the Catholic Church fearful of secularization, army officers protecting their privileged positions, and the propertied classes outraged by "communist" assaults on their wealth, the *Protocols* offered the usual antidemocratic benefits.

Since 1945 Argentina has consistently provided the largest audience, with twelve editions of the *Protocols* or *The International Jew*, the latest in 1989. During the 1970s, a conspiracy story advertised as "an application of the *Protocols of the Elders of Zion* in Argentina" gained access to the popular press. The nonexistent "Chief Rabbi

Gordon of New York City" was said to be plotting, with the help of a worldwide Zionist organization, the creation of Andinia, a Jewish republic in the state of Patagonia. Nearly a dozen "studies" of the plot appeared in book form, including extensive excerpts from the *Protocols*.

Editions of the *Protocols* in French, English, and Arabic have circulated in the Muslim world since the 1920s. That the myth of the Jewish world conspiracy should have great resonance in the Middle East is, perhaps, understandable, although far from reassuring. Here at least are real Zionists, who have the backing of Jewish and non-Jewish supporters all over the world. Here Israelis have fought victorious wars against Arab states and peoples. The *Protocols of the Elders of Zion* could make defeat more palatable, the product of the Jewish world supergovernment rather than of the relatively small State of Israel.

As in other national contexts, the forgery is most useful for leaders who seek to escape their personal responsibilities for failed policies. President Nasser of Egypt gave out copies to the foreign press corps, and in 1956, following the Suez debacle, his information service produced an edition based on a Nazi version. Several Jordanian ministers used it to explain Israel's victory in the Six Day War (1967). In 1968 King Faisal of Saudi Arabia reportedly subsidized publication of three hundred thousand copies of the *Protocols* turned out by the Beirut Islamic Institute in French, Italian, Spanish, and Arabic. President Qadaffi of Libya recommended the book as "an important and enlightening document" to Western journalists in 1972. The Kuwait postal service sent copies to postmasters all over the world in the early 1970s.

For leaders in search of exoneration, mass distribution of the *Protocols,* following the European model, is a necessity. Ominously, the diffusion of the *Protocols* has not been limited to governments that have direct political conflicts with the State of Israel. Religious and academic institutions, some of them quite distant from the Middle East, have also become involved. In Australia and Brazil, Arab-language newspapers excerpt the *Protocols*. Professors lecture on the subject in Pakistan and Algeria. Saudi Arabian religious judges distribute copies at the Consultative Assembly of the Council of Europe in Strasbourg. Ten editions of the *Protocols,* the most recent from Kirghizstan, are currently in circulation. Jews, not only Israelis, have been made the objects of hatred and suspicion to the man in the street, and the consciousness of ordinary citizens has been radically transformed. There are no known refutations of the forgery in Arabic.

Until recently, ideological antisemitism was foreign to Islam. Historically, the Jewish communities in Muslim lands, like other minority groups, suffered inferior political status, humiliating legal discrimination, and occasional violence. Before the founding of Israel, however, Jews had always played a wholly peripheral role in Islamic civilization; they were of minor importance to its theologians, philosophers, and politicians. This is no longer so. The endless theorizing about Jews, the conscious dissemination of a negative stereotype, and their placement at the very center of world evil are now also finding a place in Islamic religion and culture. The full political consequences of this change, as yet unmeasured, are cause for concern.

In spite of the Holocaust, the *Protocols of the Elders of Zion* has continued to exercise its fascination for Christian fundamentalists and the anticommunist right in the United States. As of 1992, thirty-three printings of the *Protocols, The International Jew,* or pseudo-scholarly studies of them had appeared here. Most indefatigable in keeping the forgery afloat have been the National States Rights Party, Christian Defense League, Sons of Liberty, Christian National Crusade, and the John Birch Society. Nothing, however, suggests that they have been able to gain a wide audience for the *Protocols* or to exploit its political potential. Although the myth of Jewish world conspiracy survives on the fringes of American politics, it has not entered the mainstream.

Still, two recent efforts along these lines are worth mentioning as examples of the adaptability of the *Protocols* to ever new purposes. In the 1980s Californian Noontide Press, part of the radical right network and a purveyor of extremist literature, offered the book on its list. The press maintains close connections to groups that include the Institute for Historical Review, the foremost advocate of Holocaust denial. The self-styled revisionists claim that the Holocaust never happened, that it is, in fact, the greatest "hoax of the twentieth century." Their debt to the *Protocols of the Elders of Zion* is unacknowledged but scarcely mistakable. The group's publications present Jews as engaged in a gigantic conspiracy of evil, a destructive force in past and present, worthy of hatred and fear. The *Journal of Historical Review*, once a quarterly and now a bimonthly published in California, presents itself as interested only in historical truth, but entirely in keeping with the mindset of the *Protocols*, it specializes in "unmasking" sensational conspiracies. The specific political agenda remains obscure. However, documented relations with European neo-Nazis and racists and financial support from long-time radical rightists in the United States point to the usual political orientation of those who take the *Protocols* as their inspiration.[15]

In light of current developments, the Holocaust deniers cannot be consigned to the lunatic fringe without further ado. They have recently attempted to break out of the narrow confines of America's radical right subculture to reach a more mainstream audience. Quite capable of taking advantage of every American's right to an opinion — no matter how heartless and pernicious — Holocaust deniers appear on college campuses and field questions on talk shows. They have succeeded in placing their advertisements in respectable newspapers and in posing as champions of free speech. The Holocaust deniers are also clever enough to steer clear of too close a connection to the *Protocols of the Elders of Zion*, for the forgery has an odious reputation with all but the most gullible in the audience they are now targeting. Such tactical restraint may not last, however, and it is altogether possible that Holocaust denial will win a new lease on life for the *Protocols*, as it already has for the idea of an ongoing Jewish world conspiracy.

Holocaust denial can be seen as a modern instance of the anti-democratic and antisemitic purposes that the *Protocols* has almost always served. Its appearance in a small segment of the African-American community, however, performs new functions. Black nationalists close to Louis Farrakhan and several academics independent of him have accused Jews of engaging in a range of conspiracies against African-Americans. Unnamed Jewish doctors, goes one such claim, knowingly infected blacks with the AIDS virus in order to further their plan of world domination. Another charge claims that Jews conducted the African slave trade and that the enormous wealth they thus gained is still being used to keep blacks in powerless misery.[16] According to this fable, Jewish academics, backed by an all-powerful "Jewish" media, are now busily engaged in covering up the truth. The *Protocols of the Elders of Zion,* readily obtainable in black nationalist bookstores, stands ready to integrate these separate fictions into an all-embracing historical perspective.

Familiarity with the history of the *Protocols of the Elders of Zion* can shed some light on why a few individuals in the African-American community have chosen to clothe their grievances in theories of Jewish conspiracy. Whether they are captives of the myth themselves or whether they cynically seek to use it to mobilize the following, they have noticed that an antisemitic interpretation of their problems wins the instant, emotionally charged attention of their audience in ways that more sober discussions of realities do not.

Although these individuals share none of the right's programmatic motives for propagating the *Protocols,* their readiness to engage in conspiracy thinking has undoubtedly worsened relations between American Jews and African-Americans, former allies in the struggle for civil equality. Once again overheated fantasies have obscured rather than clarified the underlying causes of conflict. Blacks have come to see Jews as part of the oppressive white power structure, as people who have made it and then slammed the door behind them. Jews feel threatened by black demands for a share in the good things of American life and have taken the campaigns of vilification by the few as representative of the many. The tragedy here is that real problems have real causes and, possibly, real solutions, none of which can be usefully addressed on the basis of myths. Sadly, antisemitism, performing its historical function, succeeds in overwhelming the expression of legitimate grievances by means of escalating rhetoric, deepening suspicion, and anger; charges and countercharges have supplanted careful, and caring, discussion.

§

While it is certain that antisemitism in general and the *Protocols of the Elders of Zion* in particular can solve no real problems, they have demonstrated the capacity to poison political life and other forms of human relations. Reasonable people have a right to be downhearted about ever conquering such a long-lived, adaptable, and serviceable lie. They have no cause to believe that the *Protocols* will soon vanish.

This brief history of the political career of the *Protocols* justifies pessimism but, perhaps, not fatalism. The forgery has not prospered everywhere to the same degree, which suggests that ways have been found to combat the evil effectively. Even though the book cannot be made to disappear, it can be driven to the fringes of a nation's political life. In closing this introduction it may be instructive to examine two attempts to render the book useless, one a relative success, the other — Binjamin Segel's — an obvious failure.

The forgery entered Great Britain from two different sources, through the agency of White Russians and through what proved to be more creditable channels. British military officers engaged in the counterrevolutionary intervention of 1918–20, English expatriates, and foreign correspondents for English newspapers returned home from Russia with a well-developed belief in Judeo-Bolshevism and possibly with versions of the *Protocols* as well. Initially, the book followed the familiar path to political relevance. Although Britain had won the war, it had strained every resource in the process. Troubles in India and Ireland were destabilizing the Empire. The demands of labor and of women, shelved during the war, were resurfacing. Bolshevism seemed to be at the point of breaking out of Russia, flooding westward.

The *Protocols* had a ready explanation for all these developments, and influential publishers, government leaders, and politicians seemed ready to make use of them. Declaring that the book could not be shrugged off, Wickham Steed of the *Times* of London called for a government investigation. The *Morning Post*, representing High Tory interests, backed the book in a series of articles, publishing them as a separate book in 1920. Winston Churchill spoke of international Jewry as the mainspring of the Russian Revolution and every subversive movement of the nineteenth century. Jews were, he wrote, practically the undisputed masters of that enormous (Russian) empire.[17]

Binjamin Segel could only register his amazement at this reception. Writing in 1924–26, he could not have known that the political importance of the *Protocols* had already peaked in England. Even though the forgery continues to appear there to the present day, it has found no meaningful political application since 1921, remaining instead the obsession of individual cranks and obscure organizations.

Key to the loss of credibility for the *Protocols* was the early and emphatic exposé done in the *Times* of London, the country's most authoritative newspaper. Discovery of the forgery's major source by one of its reporters — an event that Segel correctly saw as being of prime importance — resulted in three articles (18–20 August 1921) under the title "The End of the *Protocols*." This proved prophetic, at least in Britain. Political antisemitism continued to play its part in English public life, but the *Protocols* proved too tainted to be useful. After an initial flirtation, no responsible leaders lent their prestige to what the *Spectator* labeled "a malignant lunacy." During the 1930s, even the British Union of Fascists, a movement that found much to admire in Hitler, could find no utility in the *Protocols*.

England, however, is the exception in the otherwise gloomy history of the *Protocols of the Elders of Zion*. The more usual course of events raises several questions that Binjamin Segel and the many who came after him must have asked themselves. Why, despite several dispassionate and thorough critiques of the book and the ulterior purposes it serves, does the *Protocols* survive and prosper? What, after all, can the debunking of destructive lies accomplish? If an attempt at exposure is made, to whom should such efforts be directed? The true believer is beyond reach. The cynical propagator has no interest in truth. And the most important group to enlighten, the poorly educated whose gullibility can convert the myth into a political fact, will have little patience for minute textual criticism.

Those who would expose the forgery can turn only to the reasonably well-educated public, hoping to find there men and women of good will. Segel believed in such people and understood that the crises they were living through had caused many to question old certainties—had, in fact, created a climate in which the *Protocols,* against all reason, could exercise a destructive influence. The story of his effort to reach these people is both touching and a cautionary tale, an antidote to unwarranted optimism.

With sound credentials and the necessary expertise, Segel undertook the writing of a long scholarly study of the *Protocols of the Elders of Zion* as well as the shorter version translated here. For many years, he had done most of his writing for an organization dedicated to combating antisemitism in Germany, the Centralverein deutscher Staatsbürger jüdischen Glaubens (Central Association of German Citizens of Jewish Faith).

The Centralverein, founded in 1893, announced its position with its name. It was an organization for Jews who identified themselves wholeheartedly with the German nation, not with Jewish peoplehood. Members of the Centralverein considered themselves, and wanted others to consider them, simply as Germans of Jewish religious denomination. Their stand in favor of dignified assimilation, that is, without the sacrifice of their Judaism, spoke to the feelings of most German Jews. The Centralverein became their largest voluntary association, far exceeding the small membership of various Zionist organizations.

The Centralverein came into existence also to fight political antisemitism, which reached its pre-Nazi high point of effectiveness in the early 1890s. Antisemitism, aside from being a painful affront to loyal citizens and a stain on Germany's honor, also "impeded the full integration of Jews into the nation," as one prominent Jewish political leader had lamented.[18] To members of the Centralverein, most of whom were liberal or left-liberal in their political orientation, the duty to combat this blight was clear and the methods obvious.

Confront lies with truth; challenge libelers in the courts; and contest antisemitic political candidates wherever they appeared. In brief, give people the facts, let them discuss the issues freely, and they would come to the correct conclusions, remedy old errors, and do the right thing. Honor, not only self-defense, demanded these principles of rational politics.

In pursuance of these principles, lawyer-members of the Centralverein combed the antisemitic press looking for violations of German law. The organization published a newspaper, a journal, and dozens of books and pamphlets defending Judaism, demonstrating the service of Jews to the German state, and exposing the lies and misdeeds of the antisemites. Statistical studies, apologetics, appeals to conscience and the law were the weapons of choice.

In the years before World War I, these methods enjoyed a degree of success. Centralverein lawyers bagged several prominent antisemites and some received heavy fines and jail sentences. The fines drained the slim resources of the antisemitic political parties, while jail time for prominent leaders helped stigmatize the movement in the eyes of many respectable Germans. By 1914, the antisemitic parties had all but disappeared from German parliaments, thanks at least in part to the Centralverein.

But neither the Centralverein nor similar antidefamation organizations, which shared the same liberal philosophy, fooled themselves into believing that they had vanquished antisemitism in Germany. Their victory, limited to the antisemitic political parties, had done little to counteract the spread of antisemitism to the youth movement, the universities, or professional and cultural associations. Even the partial victory appeared to be in jeopardy during the early years of the world war, as veiled and overt antisemitic attacks managed to evade military censorship. At the close of the war and in its immediate aftermath, political antisemitism of a new and more radical stamp returned in strength. To meet this new challenge, the Centralverein relied upon the old, tried and true, methods.

In the chaotic early years of the Weimar Republic, however, fewer Germans were open to the politics of reason. Humiliation at the hands of the victorious Allies, loss of territory and resources, hunger, and inflation virtually destroyed the legitimacy of the Republic, at least for the middle- and upper-class Germans. Among these groups, the broad consensus regarding the institutions and values of prewar Germany, which the Centralverein had depended on, evaporated. When an antisemite had been convicted by the kaiser's courts, he suffered social disgrace. A few had had to withdraw from politics altogether. Now such a conviction became a badge of honor, proof that the "martyr to Jewish power" had stood up to the "Jew-Republic." In this milieu and against physical violence and the din of hysterical rhetoric, the reasonable voice of the Centralverein could not make itself heard.

Segel certainly knew that the traditional methods had lost much of their effectiveness. It was not naïveté that led him to do battle — he expresses his misgivings several times in his study of the *Protocols* — but a sense of duty to the truth. As a noncitizen, a journalist, an Eastern European Jew, he must also have known that his words would be turned on their heads by antisemites. That such a person would deny the truth of the *Protocols*, Hitler said, was the best proof of their authenticity.[19] Segel, the Centralverein, and their few non-Jewish allies were themselves seen as serving the interests of the Jewish world conspiracy.

Faced with this sort of politics, Segel, had he been a different sort of person, could have remained silent. He was already seriously ill with the disease that would kill him in 1931. But as the *Protocols* gathered strength, penetrated the universities, and recruited influential friends in high places, he could no longer wait for authoritative German Christians to speak out against the forgery. Too few of them felt personally threatened enough to overcome their disdain for the political fray. His choice then was either to allow the *Protocols* to go virtually unchallenged and to spread its poison ever more widely, or to speak out against its destructiveness, no matter how futile the gesture.

Segel probably changed few German minds about the *Protocols*, but it would have confirmed his faith in the powers of reason and his belief that no knowledge is ever truly lost to learn that his work is still being read, still instructing those willing to learn. One of its lessons is that the field must never be abandoned to the forces of ignorance and destruction.

NOTES

1. See Roberts, *Mythology of the Secret Societies*.

2. The subject certainly demands more space than can be given here. To get a better perspective on the antisemitic literary tradition to which the *Protocols* belongs, see Katz, *From Prejudice to Destruction*; Levy, ed., *Antisemitism in the Modern World*.

3. Segel's works include *Bolshewismus und Judentum* (1921; 5th ed., 1924) under the pseudonym Dmitri Bulaschow; *Die Entdeckungsreise des Herrn Dr. Theodor Lessing zu den Ostjuden* (1910), a bristling defense of Eastern European Jews against the pretensions of German Jewish "improvers"; *Der Weltkrieg und das Schicksal des jüdischen Volkes* (1915); *Die polnische Judenfrage* (1916); *Rumänien und seine Juden* (1918); and *Philosophie des Pogroms* (1923), an effective polemic against a notorious antisemitic tract, *Secessio Judaica*, by a leader and historian of the German youth movement, Hans Blüher.

4. Cited by Charles A. Ruud, "The Police and the Jewish Question in Late Imperial Russia," paper delivered before the American Association for the Advancement of Slavic Studies, Honolulu, 20 November 1993. My thanks to Jon Daly for bringing this to my attention.

5. On the issue of official complicity in antisemitic violence, see Rogger, *Jewish Policies and Right-Wing Politics in Imperial Russia*. The Union of the Russian People, founded in 1905 and known as the Black Hundreds, attempted to use anti-Jewish mob violence as a way of defending tsarism. Despite its aims, the organization had an uncertain relationship to the central government, although it may have briefly received help from low-level police agencies. In any case, no large-scale violence aimed specifically at Jews took place in Russia from 1906 until the outbreak of the civil war that followed the Revolution of 1917.

6. For a fair-minded discussion of Ford's antisemitism by a former employee, see Lee, *Henry Ford and the Jews*.

7. One of the avid proponents of the Jewish world conspiracy during the depression was Father Charles E. Coughlin, a Catholic priest. A popular radio preacher, Coughlin sermonized against international communism

and greedy capitalists, while championing a living wage for the little man. His hand-picked presidential candidate in the 1936 elections received only nine hundred thousand of forty-six million votes, but his own popularity did not diminish. In the late 1930s, when he was broadcasting over the CBS network, his large audience heard him describe antisemitism as just another variant in the crusade against communism. In March 1942 Coughlin justified Hitler's persecution of Jews as retribution for international Jewry's dragging the United States into another war against Germany. Shortly thereafter, before the federal government intervened, the Catholic Church silenced him.

Another antisemitic appeal, this time emanating from the far right, was that of Gerald L. K. Smith. Smith began his career as an aide to the populist governor of Louisiana, Huey Long, but shifted his efforts to Michigan and his politics to the defense of capitalism. He, too, made a bid for direct political influence, but his campaign for a U.S. Senate seat, first as a Republican and then as an Independent, failed miserably. Nevertheless, his magazine, *The Cross and the Flag,* and his several printings of the *Protocols,* financed by big-business figures — he claimed personal friendship with Henry Ford — disseminated his antisemitic views to a wide audience, especially in rural America. He remained a fixture in radical rightist politics until his death in 1976.

On Coughlin, see Leslie Woodcock Tentler, *Seasons of Grace: a History of the Catholic Archdiocese of Detroit* (Detroit, 1990), chapter 11. On Smith, see Levy, ed., *Antisemitism in the Modern World,* pp.160–69.

8. On Hitler's admiration for Ford, see Lee, *Henry Ford and the Jews,* pp.46, 113–14, 118.

9. See Eberhard Jäckel, ed., *Hitler: Sämtliche Aufzeichnungen, 1905–1924* (Stuttgart, 1980), p.458.

10. Hermann Rauschning, *Gespräche mit Hitler* (Zurich, 1940; repr. Vienna, 1973), pp.224–25.

11. Cited in Cohn, *Warrant for Genocide,* p.230.

12. It is true, however, that Pavolachi Krushevan, the first publisher of the *Protocols* and deeply implicated in the events at Kishinev, circulated one of the components of the myth, the so-called Rabbi's speech, before the riots.

13. Cohn, *Warrant for Genocide,* pp.169–215, 251–68.

14. R. Nudelman, "Contemporary Soviet Anti-Semitism: Form and

Content," in Theodore Freedman, ed., *Anti-Semitism in the Soviet Union: Its Roots and Consequences* (New York 1984), pp.20–21. G. Arbatov, adviser to the Politburo in the early 1970s, is the source of this speculation.

15. The most thorough treatment of this tendency is Deborah Lipstadt, *Denying the Holocaust: The Growing Assault on Truth and Memory* (New York, 1993).

16. See the definitive refutation of this myth by David Brion Davis, "The Slave Trade and the Jews," in the *New York Review of Books* 61 (22 December 1994): 14–16.

17. On Churchill, see Lebzelter, *Political Antisemitism in England*, pp.96–100. On the role of the *Morning Post*, see Holmes, "New Light on the *Protocols of Zion*," pp.13–21.

18. Ludwig Bamberger (1823–99) writing in *Deutschtum und Judentum* (Germandom and Jewry; Berlin, 1880). Excerpted in Achim von Borries, ed., *Selbstzeugnisse des deutschen Judentums* (Frankfurt, 1962), pp.18–19.

19. Adolf Hitler, *Mein Kampf*, trans. Ralph Manheim (Boston, 1943), p.307.

THE HISTORY

OF THE *PROTOCOLS*

OF THE ELDERS OF ZION

Binjamin W. Segel

THE LATEST RIDDLE OF WORLD HISTORY

Since the autumn of 1919 a remarkable book has been circulating in Germany, the civilized countries of Europe, and America, a book that lays claim to explaining—in the simplest and most natural manner—the world-shaking events of recent times and everything that pertains to them: the world war, the collapse of Russia, Bolshevism, the defeat of the Central Powers, revolution, and the overthrow of monarchy. Neither the complex interplay of social, economic, and political forces nor the jealousy of the ruling classes of individual countries, still less the errors and shortsightedness of governments, enters into this explanation. Instead, these earth-shattering upheavals that have wholly reshaped the face of the world are seen as the work of . . . *Conspiracy*. Conspirators contrived the world war, first arranging the collapse of the pillar of monarchism, Russia, and then the equally mighty support of the reigning state and social order, Germany. They elevated socialism in the shape of Bolshevism and the [Weimar] Republic to the predominant state systems in Europe. All this the insidious "concealed hand" of the conspirators accomplished, and they will not rest until the revolution has washed away all the thrones and altars of the world. Then, upon the ruins of the destroyed monarchies and Christian churches, the conspirators will erect a worldwide empire of their own.

AS INSTIGATORS OF PAST HISTORICAL UPHEAVALS

This effortless method of explaining great historical crises in "natural ways" is nothing new. Toward the end of the seventeenth century the Puritan Revolution in England was described as a conspiracy against Christianity and monarchy unleashed by "Quakers, Freethinkers, and wicked, godless Jews." "Wicked and godless Jews" were understood to be the adherents of numerous [Christian] sects who denied the Trinity, the Immaculate Conception, and other church doctrines; they were therefore reviled as Jews (even though there had been no Jews in England for centuries).

The great French Revolution of 1789 was explained in the same manner. The head of the Eudist seminary in Caën, the Abbé Barruel, did so as early as 1797 in his *Mémoire pour servir à l'histoire du Jacobinisme* [Report serving as a history of Jacobinism], and so did the Englishman Robison in *Proofs of a Conspiracy* (Edinburgh 1798). Later, the Chevalier de Malet elaborated on the entire theory "scientifically." According to him, the French Revolution and all its consequences were the fault of none other than the philosophes, the Freemasons, and the Illuminati.[1] They had conspired to overthrow the existing religions, churches, and governments of Europe. It is understandable that such a conception found the approval of the Bourbon dynasty and its supporters, whose rule came to a bloody end in 1789, for it exonerated them from the burden of any responsibility before the judgment of history. It was not their political and financial misrule or the oppression of the people or the fearsome tax burden borne by the lower classes that provoked the revolutionary catastrophe. No, it was the conspiracy of three small groups of evildoers. The French in 1789 never would have thought of rising against the hereditary royal house or of guillotining its illustrious offspring and casting off the yoke of the leading classes. Out of a pure lust for turmoil, scoundrels seduced the people away from throne and alter.

This ridiculously simplistic philosophy of history appealed to the thinking of simple people because it made no claims on their critical faculties. The most serious problems of a nation's existence could be definitively solved by means of this simple formula, which threatened to become a universally recognized truth and an ingrained, unshakable platitude to be passed on from generation to generation. Setting aside this common view of world history required the work of whole generations of critical thinkers. Their work was hindered by the defeat of Napoleon in 1815 and the restoration of the French monarchy which, in conjunction with the Holy Alliance, once again abused its power, called forth popular resistance, and spread new revolutions.

THE CONSPIRATORIAL TRINITY

Remarkably, the legend of those days did not yet identify the Jews as the guilty party. Philosophes, Freemasons, and Illuminati were the bearers of the world conspiracy. The enlightened French thinkers of the eighteenth century — the philosophes — may have helped pave the way to the revolution with their ideas, but there was nothing secret about them, and not a single one of them was Jewish. None of them were particularly interested in the Jews. Similarly, in the Masonic lodges there were no Jews upon whom to shift the whole blame for the activities of these corporations. Jews also had nothing to do with the Illuminati.

Thus the Jews remained outside consideration during the epoch of the great revolution. The French National Assembly, hesitantly and after long struggles, granted equality to the quite small number of Jews in 1791. During the first half of the nineteenth century, economic and cultural upheavals, rather than political ones, made Jewish emancipation an unavoidable necessity that even the most reactionary states had difficulty in escaping. The rising bourgeoisie of this epoch, allied to popular forces and with liberalism as its political creed, wrote Jewish emancipation on its banner. Taking up the energetic struggle for their own equality, Jews fought shoulder to shoulder with the liberals against reactionary powers. Progress, however, remained slow, and only in the 1860s was the lack of equal rights overcome in England and in Central Europe, where equality was at first more a theoretical than practical reality. In autocratic Russia the old conditions persisted until the most recent period.

In France during the Revolution of 1830 Jews remained nearly invisible. In contrast, during the Revolution of 1848 numerous Jews were active, many of them in the leading ranks. These two revolutions were pronouncedly bourgeois and not antimonarchical in character. Nevertheless, the legend of the concealed hand that crushed thrones and altars revived [in France]. Once again it was a trinity of revolutionists who brought ruin to the world. But in place of the philosophes and Illuminati stepped the Jews and Protestants. Thus, Freemasons, Jews, and Protestants, led by their Grand Master [Henry] Palmerston, the English prime minister, had engendered the revolution. Behind Palmerston stood the entire English nation, first because they were Protestants, and then because — as is well-known — the English were descended from the ten lost tribes of Israel.

The Frenchman [Henri Roger] Gougenot des Mousseaux established this theory in great detail in his book *Le Juif, le judaisme et la judaisation des peuples chrétiens* [The Jew, Judaism and the Jewification of Christian peoples; 1869].[2] This far-fetched piece of trash was republished by the Parisian antisemites in 1922 and then translated into German by the Berlin antisemites. It is a wondrous mixture of absurd fantasy, infantile politics, and pathological Jew-hatred. According to Gougenot des Mousseaux, the entire existing state system of the nineteenth century was the creation of the Jews, who took it into their heads to "Jewify" the world. As liberal demands for the rule of law, constitutionalism, separation of powers, parliamentarism, ministerial responsibility, trial by jury, social reform, and compulsory education came closer to reality, so too did the Christian world come closer to Jewification. And when all these ideals become reality, Christian Europe will abdicate and Judaism will ascend the throne.

Certain uninfluential Catholic circles responded to these views of the antediluvian knight. But the overwhelming majority of thinking Catholics everywhere rejected them with scorn. They realized correctly that the author had rendered the worst sort of disservice to their religion, portraying it as the archenemy of all freedom and political progress. A generation later, Pope Leo XIII gave the best rebuttal when he enjoined French Catholics to reconcile with the [Third French] Republic and in his encyclical *Rerum Novarum* even recognized as valid certain demands of socialism. Thereupon, Gougenot des Mousseaux and all his theories fell immediately into oblivion. They lived on only in a series of tawdry novels by the disreputable Hermann Goedsche at the end of the 1860s. They were reprinted before the world war, to the delight of sentimental flunkies and aged, thrill-seeking nannies.

Later in France and Italy and during the 1890s in Russian secret police circles (the Okhrana), the conspiracy theory was further elaborated and expanded. [In this new variant] Jews and Freemasons strove to establish a Jewish world empire on the ruins of destroyed Christian states and oppressed peoples. At its summit would rule a descendant of the Tribe of David — the incarnation of the Antichrist.[3]

A REMARKABLE BOOK OF PROTOCOLS

It would have been unnatural if, after the upheavals of 1917–18, the theory of the concealed hand had not reemerged. It did so in various books, such as [Friedrich] Wichtl's *The World War, World-Freemasonry, World Revolution*.[4] Therein it is demonstrated that the world war and revolution were unleashed by the Freemasons, among whom were many Jews in leadership positions. The most important, influential, and widely circulated of such books is the *Protocols of the Elders of Zion*. This book purports to be an authentic ancient document that indisputably proves the existence of a worldwide conspiracy. The "concealed hand" has, from time immemorial, caused wars and revolutions, leading to Bolshevism and ultimately and inevitably to the downfall of all European Christian states and of civilization itself. What we supposedly have here is not a book written by neutral observers or opponents but a report by the leaders of the conspiracy themselves, revealing their previous activity and their plans for the future. The report contains lectures delivered in twenty-four secret meetings by the chief of the supreme council of conspirators. Eventually, the Russian government, thanks to a series of incredibly crafty and daring master strokes by the Okhrana, succeeded in obtaining a copy of the lectures. In this fashion the closely guarded secrets of a world conspiracy have come to light.

The book in question is therefore of Russian origin. It is entitled *Protocols of the Elders of Zion* (also known as *Secrets of the Elders of Zion*, or in shorter form, *Zionist Protocols*). As indicated in the title, the Jews have now moved into the center of the conspiracy. In Wichtl's book they still stood in the same ranks as the Freemasons, but now the Jews have become the supreme leaders, the commanding power. The Freemasons have become their obedient slaves who blindly execute orders.

But the *Protocols* also contains the political and moral principles upon which the world conspiracy is built and through which the ends and the means to their realization are justified. The Elders of Zion, "standing at the tip of the world conspiracy and holding its bloody threads in their hands," make, as it were, a general confession that goes beyond deeds and plans to reveal their ethical principles and general philosophy. In the process, the *Protocols* sheds light on the course of recent world history in new, undreamt-of ways, unmasking the secrets of the Jews and teaching us about the essence, destiny, and goals of this nation, a people not unjustly described as a "world riddle."

WHAT WE LEARN FROM THE *PROTOCOLS*

Before going into the *Protocols* in depth, let us proceed with a brief overview of its contents:

The Jews have constituted a worldwide secret conspiratorial society that seeks to bring down all thrones and altars, set aside all monarchs, and destroy all states. On the ruins they will erect a Jewish world empire ruled by an absolute monarch of unprecedented power, an autocrat out of the House of David. To attain these ends, the Jews employ the services of the secret world organization of Freemasons. They are completely subject to the power of the Jews, a blind tool in their hands; without a will of their own, they merely carry out orders in servile obedience. To destroy empires and annihilate peoples, the Jews hatch revolutions, which in turn bring the principles and institutions of liberalism to the fore.

These are: equality of all citizens before the law, freedom of conscience and religion, freedom of the press, compulsory education,
universal suffrage, constitutional government, parliamentarism,
separation of powers, ministerial responsibility, and the like. Liberalism leads inevitably to socialism and then to anarchism and Bolshevism, whereby the states must finally and irreparably perish. All
revolutions of this type, and especially the great French Revolution,
are the work of the Jews and their helpers, the Freemasons.

WHO RULES THE WORLD?
Once again, it is the Jews who ruin the different classes of people in
the Christian states, inciting them to mutual hatred, envy, and discord. Class war is an invention of the Jews, and it is the Jews who
oversee its constant renewal. It is the Jews who incite the workers
into demanding high wages, who foment the lesser and greater
strikes. Meanwhile they bring about constantly rising prices for the
essentials, and they lure workers into drunkenness. Thus, in spite of
higher wages, which ruin non-Jewish industry, the workers never
achieve security but instead sink into yet greater misery and into
servitude to the Jews. Long ago Jews robbed the non-Jewish aristocracy of its political influence. Today they are taking away its
landed estates by encouraging prodigality and dissipation while
simultaneously raising the land tax to astronomical levels.

These internal policies of the Jews are complemented by their
foreign policy. Of course, it is the Jews who turn the states, empires,
and peoples against one another and who bring on devastating wars,
such as the most recent world war. Jews are responsible for spreading the world's great epidemics, famines, and other plagues—all
with the design of undermining Christian peoples and their states so
as to inherit their glory.

THE BACKGROUND OF THE WORLD WAR
The Assembly of the Elders of Zion—the supreme executive council of the entire Jewish nation—constitutes the *secret supreme government of the world,* to which all the world's governments are subject.
When necessary, the secret supreme government exercises its domi-

nation through ruthless acts of terror, for example, the assassination of high personages with bombs or guns. Assassination arouses feelings of helpless dread, making it easy for the supreme government to work its will. All past murders of princes and, more recently, those of Tsar Alexander II, other leading princes, and the heir-apparent to the Austrian throne in June 1914 are the work of the secret Jewish supreme government.[5] In more peaceful times the Jewish supreme government operates through bribery. The Elders of Zion have at their disposal the entire gold reserves of the world, and they boast: "In two days time we can raise from our secret vaults any quantity of gold desired."

As already mentioned, for decades before its outbreak in 1914, the world war had been quietly prepared by this supreme world government of the Elders of Zion, which systematically stirred up national strife, mutual envy, and jealousy among the nations. The world war led to the destruction of Russia and the establishment of the communist Soviet state by the Jews. Then the German monarchy was done away with, again by the Jews. Between these two occurrences there transpired an event of world-shaking significance: England's establishment of the Zionist Jewish state in Palestine through the Balfour Declaration of November 1917.[6] This could never have happened without the destruction of Russia and Germany, the two main pillars of the monarchical and Christian state order in Europe.

The Jewish state in Palestine is not the final goal of Jewish greed. It is only to be the personal headquarters and base of the Jewish masters of the world, or, more accurately, the strategic political antechamber for the coming Jewish world empire and its Jewish sovereign master. The world empire shall be founded as soon as the Jewish world government in Moscow has succeeded in making world revolution a reality. It is superfluous to emphasize that the first victim of world revolution will be the German Republic, where the Jews will introduce communism and Bolshevism according to the Russian model. Germany will then be annexed to the Jewish world empire.

As soon as the Jews have founded their world empire and crowned their world master, there will not be a communist, socialist, or even a constitutional state. No! No one in the world so thoroughly hates liberalism and all the "isms" that flow from it as the Elders of Zion! They have drummed these erroneous doctrines and false slogans into the stupid goyim[7] only as long as it is necessary to undermine their states from within and to plunge them into the abyss. But no one knows better than the Elders of Zion that the true happiness of men does not lie in the proclamation of revolutionary principles such as freedom of conscience or universal equality. Therefore, the most characteristic element of their legislation will be the demand for unconditional obedience to authority. They will, without mercy, execute those who take up arms against their government. They will immediately institute a bloodbath among their loyal coconspirators, the Freemasons who have been privy to all their secret plottings. Most will be exterminated by the sword; the survivors will be sent to penal colonies overseas.

The world empire established by the Elders of Zion will look much like the empire of Nicholas I. It will be governed with the same means used by Ivan the Terrible.[8] Under no circumstances will education be made compulsory. That was one of the most dangerous policies that the Freemasons, on Jewish orders, pursued among the stupid goyim. Universal education among the lower classes has contributed most of all to the decline of the Christian states. In the world empire of the Elders of Zion, it will be the highest duty of the loyal subject to render service as spy and informer. A wholly new economic policy will also be introduced; its hallmarks will be abolition of the stock exchange and the gold standard for currency. The gold standard was ruinous to all the states that adopted it, and that is why the Jews and Freemasons have spared no efforts to push through the gold standard for Christian states. Such ruin will be avoided at all costs in their own world empire. So, too, the stock exchange, which serves only to ruin Christian states, will be abolished in their state.

[Paradoxically,] the Elders of Zion will in this way restore true well-being and individual freedom to a deranged world. Then will they address the nations: "Praise God and bend your knee before the Chosen of God—the Jewish world master. From his exalted countenance beams forth the Providence of world history." It will be the Jewish world master's highest claim to fame that he has broken the senseless revolutionary forces that arise from the bestial instincts rather than human reason. These same forces are now celebrating their triumph under the guise of freedom and law, when in reality all is robbery and violence. They have destroyed the social order.

§

ORIGINS OF THE *PROTOCOLS*

These Jewish plans for the conquest and deliverance of the world were supposedly developed in August 1897 at the first Zionist Congress, convened by Theodor Herzl in Basel [Switzerland]. Although age-old, the plans received their final formulation by Herzl. In twenty-four secret sessions at the congress, he reported on them to an audience of selected conspirators.[9] A Russian government spy was sent there to record what was said. A copy of his report was given to Professor Sergei A. Nilus, a Russian scholar in Moscow. A full eight years later, in the autumn of 1905, [Nilus] published it in the Russian language under the title "Protocols of the Assembly of the Elders of Zion," as an appendix to the second edition of his work *The Great in the Small, or the Advent of the Antichrist and the Approaching Rule of the Devil on Earth* (1st ed., 1901). Nilus published this book in three further editions (1911, 1912, 1917), and each time the "Protocols" appendix was enlarged by introductions, footnotes, and afterwords. Each time the narrow framework of the "Protocols" was expanded, while the general picture remained the same.

HOW THE PROTOCOLS SURFACED IN GERMANY

In Germany the *Protocols* was introduced in the autumn of 1919, about a year after the [German] revolution, by a Herr Gottfried zur Beek (whose real name is Captain [Ludwig] Müller von Hausen).[10] He published it in his extensive work *Die Geheimnisse der Weisen von Zion* [The secrets of the Elders of Zion, pp.68–143]. The translation alleges to be from the 1911 edition [of Nilus's book].

However, zur Beek's work is not at all the same as Nilus's, and the reader learns nothing of the contents or even of the existence of Nilus's book. Nor does the reader learn that the *Protocols,* which forms the crux of zur Beek's book, was only an appendix in [Nilus's] Russian text. Moreover, zur Beek fills his book to overflowing with [his own] notes, analogies, illustrations, and documentation, which are supposed to authenticate the *Protocols* and prove the existence of the Jews' plan for world conquest. The most significant added documents are the "Rabbi's Speech Concerning the Goyim," dating from 1901, and the speech of another rabbi supposedly delivered to the Zionist Congress of Lwow in 1912. With only minor variations, both speeches further developed the Jewish plan of conquest. Zur Beek's lavishly produced book was grandiosely dedicated to "the princes of Europe," and it warned of the threatening danger to throne and altar posed by the Jewish world conspiracy.

WHO UNDERTOOK THE PROTECTION OF THE *PROTOCOLS?*
Zur Beek's work had powerful aristocratic sponsors. Prince Otto zu Salm-Horstmar and Count Behr, the former chairman of the Conservative Party in the Prussian upper house, had, as it was later discovered, contributed quite considerable sums for both a popular and a fancy edition. High aristocratic circles backed vigorous publicity for dissemination of the work to all parts of the population, especially in the countryside and the provinces. Prince Joachim Albrecht of Prussia personally bestowed copies on the waiters and servants of the luxury hotels and restaurants he frequented. Kaiser Wilhelm II recommended it to all his visitors at Doorn, where individual chapters were read aloud to dinner guests.[11] Incessantly, the conservative press printed new detailed reports and commentary on the world conspiracy of the Jews, finally come to light. [The Jewish conspiracy] explained the world-shattering events of recent decades "in the simplest and most natural way."

THE MOST WIDELY DISTRIBUTED BOOK IN THE WORLD
From Berlin, the *Protocols* made virtually a triumphal procession through the civilized countries of Europe and on to America. Al-

most simultaneously with the Berlin editions there appeared a Polish version in Warsaw, then in quick succession three French translations in Paris, an English version in London, and three further in New York. Editions in Scandinavia, Italy, and Japan [in Russian] followed. In the summer of 1925 a complete Arabic translation appeared in Damascus and immediately achieved wide circulation. The Latin patriarch of Jerusalem made effective propaganda for it throughout the Orient. The prohibition of the book by the French High Commissioner of Syria only contributed to its popularity. All of the mentioned translations included detailed introductions, comments, and explanations, only part of which came from zur Beek's work. It can be said with confidence that no piece of modern literature has even approximated the circulation of the *Protocols*.

The *Times* of London sounded an alarm, demanding a public inquiry into the secret world conspiracy of the Jews. Among other things, that newspaper wrote:

What are these "Protocols"? Are they authentic? If so, what malevolent assembly concocted these plans, and gloated over their exposition? Are they a forgery? If so, whence comes the uncanny note of prophecy, prophecy in parts fulfilled, in parts far gone in the way of fulfilment? Have we been struggling these tragic years to blow up and extirpate the secret organization of German world dominion only to find beneath it another, more dangerous because more secret? Have we, by straining every fibre of our national body, escaped a "Pax Germanica" only to fall into a "Pax Judaica"? (8 May 1920)

This quotation aptly illustrates the unusually strong impression the *Protocols* has made upon the leading intellects of English public life. The world-renowned London newspaper perceives in the "Jewish world conspiracy" a power equal to that of Germany, the defeat of which required the cooperation of several great states. The *Morning Post* [London] devoted twenty-three long leaders to the question, which aroused enormous interest throughout the British Empire; it soon came out in book form under the title *The Cause of World Unrest*. After a special American edition, sales of the book were rapid on both sides of the ocean.

Polish-Americans, embarrassed by the anti-Jewish pogroms[12] in their liberated fatherland, distributed pamphlets in both North and South America in English and Portuguese. They referred to the newly discovered *Protocols* to show that the Polish pogroms were only defensive actions against the Jewish world conspiracy that had already destroyed Russia with Jewish Bolshevism and was now reaching out toward Poland. Should this bulwark of Christianity be torn down, world revolution would flood unhindered into the rest of Europe and into America. During the summer of 1920, when the Red Army stood at the gates of Warsaw, the entire Polish episcopate called upon the bishops of the whole Catholic world with an appeal very much in line with the thinking of the *Protocols*. (It will be remembered that the *Protocols* had been translated into Polish in early 1920, in fact, by an Assumptionist father named Evrard, whose name, however, did not appear on the title page.)

In England the Britons, a nationalist-racist organization, and in America the automobile king and multimillionnaire Henry Ford, established their own periodicals to spread knowledge of the *Protocols*. [Ford's] *Dearborn Independent* soon numbered three hundred thousand subscribers. The paper's long-winded commentaries appeared in a four-volume book that circulated in a half million copies.

Theodor Fritsch of Leipzig published [an abridged two-volume] German translation of [Ford's] book as *Der internationale Jude*. By the beginning of 1922 it was already in its twenty-first printing. Whole carloads of the book were dispatched to Hungary and Romania. In 1924 Fritsch published in German *Die zionistischen Protokolle: Das Programm der internationalen Geheimregierung* [The Zionist Protocols: the program of the international secret government], a translation of the English version of the *Protocols,* with his own preface and afterword. The eighty-page pamphlet was soon distributed in tens of thousands of copies.[13] *Schuldbuch Judas* [The account book of Judah] by "Wilhelm Meister" [Paul Bang], relying on the *Protocols,* achieved a circulation of 150,000. A book of commentary by Alfred Rosenberg sold approximately fifty thousand. Zur Beek's book sold approximately 120,000. Excerpts and summaries of the *Protocols* were disseminated in countless pamphlets.

Before Easter 1925 an anonymous society calling itself the Initiates of Vienna published a splendidly printed edition of the *Protocols,* replete with a detailed introduction, many scholarly footnotes, and an extensive index. It reached new highs in circulation during the Zionist Congress in Vienna in August 1925.

THE EFFECTIVENESS OF
THE *PROTOCOLS* AMONG THE EDUCATED

Meanwhile, the general public's belief in the *Protocols* struck deep roots. Scholarly historians gave countless lectures on the Jewish world conspiracy to educated audiences of former military men, officials, cultured ladies, and especially university students. These lectures harked back to medieval religious disputations. Passions were whipped up to fever heat. The audience had put before it the embodiment and the cause of all evil, the instigators of the war, the authors of the defeat, the makers of the revolution — in short, those responsible for all the misery that has come over us. It was possible to lay hands on this enemy, yet he skulked in the shadows. What might he be plotting now? — a frightening thought.

To observe these students was remarkable. A few hours before, perhaps under the guidance of a world-famous scholar, they were straining their intellects searching for the solution to legal, philosophical, or mathematical problems. Now, however, their young blood was seething, their eyes blazing, fists clenched, voices hoarse with shouts of approval, outrage, and calls for vengeance. Often debate was permitted, but whoever dared to express a slight doubt would be shouted down as a lackey of the Jews, a Social Democrat, or a Bolshevik and might even be physically threatened. Were a Jew recognized in the audience, he would find it difficult to escape with his skin.

GENERAL LUDENDORFF
LENDS HIS SUPPORT TO THE *PROTOCOLS*

The various translations of the *Protocols* reached new heights in large editions. At each new [Reichstag] election in Germany, the *Protocols* proved to be the most effective weapon against the "Jew-Republic."

Pamphlets and newspaper articles treating the theme in popular fashion multiplied, enlightening the masses as to the plans of the Jews. Now General [Erich] Ludendorff has thrown the full weight of his authority behind belief in the existence of the Jewish plan for world conquest.[14] In the third volume of his book, *Kriegführung und Politik* [War and politics, p.322], he writes: "Recently, publications discussing the position of the Jewish people have increased in number. The German people, but other peoples of the earth as well, have good reason to concern themselves with the historical development, organizations, fighting methods, and plans of the Jewish people. [Were we to do this,] it is to be assumed that, in many instances, we would be inclined to write world history differently."

In a separate footnote, General Ludendorff emphatically recommends to those readers who "want to gain an independent judgment" that they consult Gottfried zur Beek's book. Again, from Ludendorff's *War and Politics* (p.511): "Hand in hand with France and England worked the High Command of the Jewish people. Perhaps it directed both countries. It saw the approaching war as a means to put through its political and economic aims: the acquisition of a national territory in Palestine, recognition as a nation, and the creation of a hegemony in the politics and capitalist economies of Europe and America."

As is apparent, General Ludendorff here confesses his complete faith in the *Protocols*. It is not difficult to see that this confession of faith from the famed field marshal added powerfully to the repute of the *Protocols* and that it also spread zur Beek's work into previously inaccessible circles.

§

ON THE TRACK OF A FORGERY

As early as May 1920 the Berlin monthly *Im deutschen Reich* [In the German empire] published a devastating critique of zur Beek's book. In it Dr. J. Stanjek demonstrated that the "Jewish plan of world conquest" in the *Protocols* was remarkably similar to the one developed by the infamous Hermann Goedsche, mentioned previ-

ously. Who was Goedsche? An extraordinary, obscure gentleman —
a journalist of the gutter press. In 1848 he played a tawdry role in the
trial for high treason of the democratic leader [Benedikt] Waldeck,
the father of the Prussian Constitution [of 1848]. He lent his hand
to a forgery that attempted to impugn the moral and political reputation of this honest man. [Upon discovery of the fraud] Goedsche
was dismissed from his job as a postal official. He became an editor
of the *Kreuzzeitung* [a conservative Berlin newspaper] and published a great number of novels, historical potboilers of a poetic
strain, under the pseudonym Sir John Retcliffe, thereby trying to
pass himself off as an English diplomat.

One of these novels, *Biarritz*, appeared in 1868 with a chapter
entitled "In the Jewish cemetery of Prague." There it was described
how in the gloom of night the princes of the twelve tribes of Israel
gathered from all the capitals of Europe at the grave of a Jewish holy
man. One after another they reported the progress of an ancient
plan of world conquest in their respective realms, how far the subjection of the goyim had proceeded, and what remained yet to be
done. This plot bore such a striking resemblance to the one developed in the *Protocols* that any reasonable person must conclude that
*either both were written by the same man or one was plagiarized from
the other*.

WHERE DID THE *PROTOCOLS* GET ITS INFORMATION?
Stimulated by the findings of Stanjek's clear-sighted article, Otto
Friedrich, the Social Democratic writer, undertook a thorough
comparison of Goedsche's novel and the *Protocols*. Placing the first
rabbi's speech from zur Beek next to Goedsche's speech of the Jewish tribal princes, [Friedrich] demonstrated to every literate person
that the two intellectual products were nearly identical, even in their
phrasing.

The first rabbi's speech was adopted by the antisemites in 1901
and became a staple weapon in their "intellectual" arsenal. The
second rabbi's speech is nothing more than a watered-down version
of [Goedsche], put into the mouth of a rabbi at the Lwow Zionist

Congress of 1912—a congress that never took place. Since 1913, this speech has achieved equal importance in the writings of the antisemites. In zur Beek's book, both versions are to be found peacefully coexisting and bearing witness to the Jews' plans of world conquest and the authenticity of the *Protocols*. Friedrich branded this "the book of forgeries."

Also working from Stanjek's article, the famed Orientalist, theologian, and member of the Protestant consistory, Professor Hermann Strack of Berlin University dealt with the *Protocols* in the seventh edition (1921) of his *Jüdische Geheimgesetze?* [Secret laws of the Jews?]. Concisely and definitively, he passed a crushing, annihilating judgment. In an addendum, Strack was able to include the latest finding of Philip Graves, the *Times* of London correspondent in Constantinople, a discovery that confirmed Stanjek's acute insights.

Stanjek had hypothesized that the author of the *Protocols* had plagiarized several passages from a French book that predated the fall of the Second Empire [1870]. The *Times* correspondent wrote three lead articles (16–18 August 1921) about a well-thumbed, untitled little book that he had acquired in Constantinople from a Russian refugee, a former Okhrana operative. In it the journalist found an extraordinary number of excerpts from the later *Protocols*. It was soon established that the book was *Dialogue aux enfers entre Machiavel et Montesquieu* [Dialogue between Machiavelli and Montesquieu in Hell], a scabrous satire on the usurper Napoleon III. Maurice Joly, a Parisian lawyer, first published the book anonymously in 1865 and then under his own name in Brussels in 1868.[15]

Thus the world-conquering plans of the Elders of Zion came out of Goedsche's trashy novel. But the Elders' political dogmas and schemes, as well as the moral principles that were their foundation, came almost word for word from the speeches of Machiavelli in Joly's petty satire on Napoleon III. Now there were two sources from which the Elders of Zion must have fashioned their wisdom. Later, we shall deal with the plagiarisms in detail and, by means of textual comparison with the original, we shall make the thefts clear.

These findings fell far short of shaking the general belief in the authenticity of the *Protocols*. Antisemitic propagandists make much of the difference between plagiarism and falsification. Proving plagiarism does not necessarily mean that falsification has taken place. First of all, the antisemites claim, it must be shown who did the plagiarizing. Who else but the Elders of Zion? Bent on world conquest and autocratic rule, they naturally stole from wherever they could, including Machiavelli and even [Konstantin] Pobodonostev, the well-known fanatical defender of tsarism and the Russian Orthodox Church. In Joly [the Elders] found a beautifully developed theory for political usurpation and fiendishly clever violation of nations. Why not make use of all this?

Hermann Goedsche had had exact knowledge of the Jewish plan for world conquest and had rendered it poetically in his writing. It was even asserted that none other than Ferdinand Lassalle had been the one who initiated Goedsche into the deepest secrets of the Jews.[16] The similarity between the plans in the *Protocols* and those of Goedsche just went to prove that the Jewish world conspiracy had existed for a long time. Plans of world conquest, of course, had to be adapted to new conditions by every new generation. As far as concerns Maurice Joly, Lord Alfred Douglas, the London antisemitic leader, disclosed in his journal *Plain English* (27 August 1921) that [Joly] was a Jew, circumcised as Moses Joel. Lord Douglas claims to have discovered this in the obscure memoirs of a French government official, who was supposedly "intimately acquainted with revolutionaries and their Jewish wire-pullers."

MAURICE JOLY, THE "JEWISH" REVOLUTIONARY
This discovery put a whole new face on the affair. "Moses Joel" was a Jewish revolutionary, a communist, and a forerunner of Trotsky, as well as the Elders of Zion.[17] Zur Beek, in the preface to the eighth edition of his book (31 August 1923), writes: "He [Joly] is, in fact, a precursor of the Elders of Zion and affords us an excellent look into the art of Jewish conspiracy. The author of this dialogue, Joly-Joel, prepared the downfall of the house of Bonaparte and the rising

of the Commune of 1871."[18] There are two versions of Joly's end. The first has him dying on the barricades [during the Commune of Paris]. The other claims a suitable death for the Jewish communist — suicide.

Joly "naturally" interwove into his book the plans of Jewish world conquest. Small wonder that the Elders of Zion should incorporate them in their own *Protocols*. Count [Ernst zu] Reventlow, the advocate in Germany of this theory in numerous articles and brochures, identifies [the plagiarist of Joly] as either Theodor Herzl, the founder of political Zionism, or his foremost opponent, the Hebrew writer Ahad Ha'am.[19] One or the other allegedly addressed the twenty-four secret sessions at the end of August 1897 in Basel.

§

THE STRANGE ATTITUDE OF GERMAN SCIENCE

It is strange that the entire German scientific establishment remains silent. It stands by as the belief in the genuineness of the *Protocols* and the existence of a Jewish world conspiracy sinks ever deeper roots among the educated classes of the German people. Thus today [the myth] is almost ineradicable. None of the great German scholars renowned for textual criticism has exerted himself to unmask the fraud and drive the authors from the temple. Professor Strack is the only exception, but many years ago his stand against the "blood libel" earned him, not praise as a lover of truth, but condemnation as a lackey of the Jews.[20] Now and then a serious journal such as the *Christliche Welt* [Christian world] has raised a few prosaic doubts. But such voices have been drowned out in the general din.

Professor Ulrich Karstädt of Göttingen University asserts that a thorough refutation, one that would stand up in court, would require the disagreeable, rigorous, and endlessly troublesome textual comparison of the Russian original, the translations that issued from it, and all the many introductions, afterwords, and commentaries attached to the *Protocols*. I have undertaken to do this in my book *Die Protokolle der Weisen von Zion, kritisch beleuchtet* (Berlin,

1924) [The Protocols of the Elders of Zion, critically illuminated], in order to settle accounts with this fabrication once and for all, scientifically and objectively. [Working from all four editions of Nilus's work and several translations of it, including the commentaries,] I have collected enough material to serve as the basis for an investigation of the *Protocols*.[21]

IN WHAT LANGUAGE WAS THE ORIGINAL TEXT WRITTEN?

As we have seen, the *Protocols of the Elders of Zion* came to us in the Russian version of Sergei A. Nilus, who claimed to have translated it. The question arises: from what language did Nilus translate? Zur Beek assures us, short and to the point: "The original text was in French." However, that assertion rings untrue given that the language of the proceedings at the First Zionist Congress of 1897, at which the *Protocols* was supposedly delivered, was German. As can be seen from the printed official record, even the speeches given in Russian had to be translated into German. All the delegates understood German, although not all of them could speak it. The only delegate whose mother tongue was French also spoke in German. How then can it be believed that the original text of the *Protocols* was French? Nilus, unfortunately, utters not a word as to the original language in all his introductions and commentaries.

According to another variant, advanced by Theodor Fritsch in the preface to his edition, the original language was Hebrew, the text being confiscated by the Russian police during a house search in St. Petersburg. They delivered the manuscript to the scholarly Professor Nilus for translation into Russian. Nilus could have saved everyone much trouble had he published the original alongside his translation. For example, had the original been in French, three different Frenchmen would not have had to retranslate it into French. Had it been Hebrew, Nilus had the duty to publish the original manuscript, as is the custom among Orientalists. Nilus could have settled the whole regrettable argument about the authenticity of the *Protocols* by publishing a facsimile of the original, or even part of it. It might have then been possible to gain some insight as to the authors and the origins of the manuscript.

The origins of the *Protocols* remain as murky as the question of the original language. Quite a few theories have been reported. According to Gottfried zur Beek, at the end of August 1897, an emissary of the Elders of Zion brought the manuscript of the twenty-four secret sessions from Basel to a Masonic lodge in Frankfurt am Main. On the way, he stayed overnight in a little town where there waited a Russian spy with his team of scribes. Bribed by the spy, [the emissary] handed over the manuscript, whereupon the scribes copied as much as they could. This copy was then reproduced and delivered to Russia's leading men, among them Professor Nilus and his co-publisher, G. V. Butmi.

Theodor Fritsch specifies two variants. In the first (already mentioned), the government delivered the confiscated Hebrew manuscript of the *Protocols* to Nilus in 1901. Fritsch contributes another version in a footnote to his translation of Ford's book, *The International Jew*. The Hebrew text of the *Protocols,* he says, existed in Russia in the 1890s; it was translated into French and taken to be read out to the Zionist Congress in Basel in 1897. A copy of the French translation made it to Paris in the same year and was then transmitted by [Pyotr] Rachkovsky, chief of the foreign branch of the Russian police in Paris, to the Russian minister of the interior.[22]

Nilus himself declared in the epilogue to his [1905] edition of the *Protocols*: "These Protocols were secretly extracted from a whole book of protocols by my correspondents, who removed the entire text from the Zionist executive archives, located on French territory." In the introduction to his 1911 edition, Nilus says:

In 1901 a now deceased acquaintance, Court Marshal Alexei Sukhotin of Tchernigov, gave into my possession a handwritten manuscript that detailed completely and clearly the secret Jewish-Freemason conspiracy that will surely lead to the end of our vile world. The person who gave me this manuscript assured me that it was a faithful translation of the original document. It had been stolen by a lady from one of the highest and most influential leaders of the Freemasons following a secret meeting somewhere in France, that hotbed of Masonic conspiracy.

Roger Lambelin's French translation from the 1912 edition of Nilus brings yet another version to the fore. The *Protocols* was purloined from an iron chest in a town in Alsace, certainly by the wife or the lover of the aforementioned Masonic leader.

What Nilus has to say in the 1917 edition is especially important:

My book with all the Protocols is now appearing in its fourth edition, but now for the first time I have learned from authoritative Jewish sources that the *Protocols* is nothing less than the strategic plan of world conquest whereby the world will be brought under Israel's yoke, the enemy of God. The plan, worked out by the leaders of the Jewish people during the many centuries of the Diaspora, was finally disclosed to the Elders by the Prince of the Exile, Theodor Herzl, at the time of the first Zionist Congress in Basel (August 1897).

Lamentably, Nilus does not betray his authoritative sources. But we learn from his words that before 1917 he had had no inkling of any connection between Basel, Herzl, or the Zionist Congress and the *Protocols*. Until 1917, his *Protocols* had not the slightest to do with the Herzl Zionists of Basel. Zur Beek, who tells us the fanciful story that his translation is from the 1911 edition [of Nilus] is, therefore, obviously lying.

Nilus says more about the origins of the *Protocols*:

In 1901, when I came into possession of the manuscript, it was like the miracle of a blind man seeing again. The manuscript was titled *Protocols of the Elders of Zion,* and I received it from the late leader of the Tchernigov nobility, Alexander Nikolaievich Sukhotin. He related to me that he had obtained it from a lady, an expatriate. He told me her name, but I have forgotten it. . . . He said that this lady had received the manuscript in a somewhat mysterious way, by theft, I believe. . . . When I became acquainted with the contents of the manuscript, I was convinced that its horrible cruelty, its implacable truthfulness, bore witness to its true origins — the Elders of Zion.

Thus, Nilus would have us believe, the origins of the manuscript are a matter of no great importance; the horrifying contents alone suffice to show that it emanated from the Elders of Zion. Nilus doesn't seem to realize that we only learn from the *Protocols* itself that there were Elders of Zion and that the *Protocols* was their work.

Still, he continues to inform us about the origins of the mysterious manuscript: "It has not been established in what ways this document, containing the holiest of Israel's ambitions and the centuries-old mystery of its leaders, made its way into the world of the uninitiated. As already mentioned, it was handed over to me in 1901. In that year, Theodor Herzl confirmed in circular no.18 that certain confidential information, despite stern warning to the contrary, had not remained secret but had rather been given undesirable publicity." Nilus instructs us in this way that the mysterious lady's theft of the manuscript was perpetrated against none other than the author of the *Protocols,* Theodor Herzl, and not until 1901. It was this "indiscretion" Herzl was supposedly bemoaning in circular no.18. Unfortunately, no person other than Nilus has seen this circular no.18, nor has anyone else ever heard of it. But on the basis of Nilus's information, it is clear that what zur Beek says concerning the origin of the manuscript, as well as the time it supposedly fell into Nilus's hands, is a total lie.

The Polish translator simplifies the matter significantly. On the first page of his introduction to the second edition of 1923, he writes: "On the origins of the book we know nothing more than what Nilus tells us, namely that the *Protocols* was stolen from the home of the founder of Zionism, Theodor Herzl."

Monsignor Jouin mentions this version but also adds another whereby the *Protocols* was put together from lecture notes of Jewish students in Paris in 1901. Unfortunately, we do not learn where the lectures were given or where the notes were made.

Herman Bernstein adds the information that the secret iron chest containing the manuscript of the *Protocols* was supposedly situated in a small town in Switzerland.[23]

INSOLUBLE CONTRADICTIONS

G. V. Butmi, one of Nilus's close associates, published the *Protocols* in 1907 as part of his work *The Enemies of the Human Race,* an exposé of the Freemasons. In his introduction Butmi states:

The *Protocols* was obtained with the greatest difficulty and translated into Russian in December 1901. It is almost impossible to get back into the secret archive in which it is concealed. It is therefore not possible to determine where and when it was composed. The reader who is more or less familiar with the secrets of the Freemasons will, however, conclude from the criminal character of the revealed plans that they are genuine and will, with great certainty, recognize that the documents emanate from the Masonic lodge of the Egyptian rite (Mizraim), most of whose members are Jews.

From these lines we learn that the *Protocols* has nothing to do with the Zionist Congress convened by Herzl in Basel in 1897. Rather, it is the work of Freemasons belonging to the Mizraim lodge. We also learn from Butmi that the *Protocols* was removed with great difficulty from a hiding place on French soil. He states this even more clearly in his conclusion: "The above *Protocols* are signed by the representatives of Zion, not to be confused with the representatives of the Zionist movement. They originate from an entire book of protocols that the translator did not have time to copy in their entirety. They originate from the secret archives of the main office of Zion, which stands in French territory." Butmi's rendition wholly contradicts that of Nilus. He emphatically denies that the *Protocols* stands in any relationship to Herzl or the Basel congress. (We will see below the reasons for this explicit declaration.) The "Zion" of Butmi is apparently quite different from the Zion of the Zionists. What Butmi has in common with Nilus is the date 1901, the removal of the manuscript, and its secret source.

All these assertions, as is apparent, fail to illuminate the origins and date of composition of the *Protocols*. In fact, they further confuse the issue. Nilus adds the following in his 1905 edition: "With such criminal undertakings, direct proofs cannot be expected. We must be satisfied, however, by the clear and compelling circumstantial evidence that will fill every Christian observer with outrage."

In the 1911 edition, Nilus expresses this thought more forcefully: "The educated non-Jewish reader will see in his daily life and in the lightning-like events that have struck Russia and all of Europe a fullness of evidence for the authenticity of the *Protocols*. Whoever can think logically will soon be convinced of its genuineness."

Roger Lambelin says: "The Russian translators are both honorable, devout men." Monsignor Jouin asserts: "The authenticity of the *Protocols* is vouched for by the good faith of the two translators. They assure us that they have worked from the French original. We know their names: S. Nilus and G. Butmi. Furthermore, their translations agree with one another."

It's a shame, however, that their pronouncements concerning the origin of the *Protocols* agree so little!

THE BOOK WITH NO FIRST EDITION

In what year did the book first appear? We still have no answer to this question. Zur Beek assures us categorically that "the first edition of the minutes of the Elders' meetings appeared in 1902." A few lines later he says that in the same year there appeared in St. Petersburg another edition entitled *The Root of Our Evil,* with no editor's name. Jouin repeats all this, and Lambelin racks his brains over whether or not a second edition was published in 1903. Zur Beek brazenly claims that the edition of 1902 is in his possession. If true, then zur Beek has the copy of a book that does not exist, that never existed, and that no mortal man has ever seen, touched, or weighed.

Nilus writes in 1911 that the *Protocols* first saw the light of day in the second edition of his book *The Great in the Small,* that is, toward the end of 1905. The first edition of this book, which did not contain the *Protocols,* appeared in 1901. It is inconceivable that Nilus should have waited so long to publish this dreadful manuscript. [Segel points out that, had Nilus possessed the manuscript in 1901 or in 1897, as the lying zur Beek maintains, then he would surely have published it sooner than 1905, the date he himself provides.]

THE WORLD'S STRANGEST BOOK

Alas, all these introductions, afterwords, and commentaries tell us just as little about the first edition of the *Protocols* as they do about the origins and language of its composition. We have before us what must be a singular phenomenon in world literature. A most strange book exists. It has been translated into all major languages. It has been massively distributed throughout the world and endlessly commented upon. Numberless articles for and against it have been written. And yet no one knows the author, its original language, when or where it was written, and how it was unearthed. None can say with absolute certainty where and when it was first published. Nobody can even boast of having seen a copy of the first edition. We are not speaking of a work from gray antiquity, written in hieroglyphics and found in some Egyptian pyramid or on cuneiform tablets from the treasure chamber of an Assyrian king. No, the book was written scarcely a generation ago in one of two languages spoken and written by several million Europeans. The originator Nilus, with whose name the book is connected, lives among us today in the city of Kiev, a few hours by plane from Vienna or Berlin.

To bring into harmony all the various, contradictory assertions, there is only one thing left for us to do. We must accept all of them as true. Just as Homer was said to have been born in seven Greek cities simultaneously, so Nilus translated the *Protocols* from the French and the Hebrew simultaneously. They originated at the Basel Zionist Congress of 1897 and, at the same time, in the lecture notes of Paris students. They were stolen by a noblewoman of Tchernigov from a high Masonic dignitary and, at the same time, by this dignitary's wife or lover. This lady gave it to Nilus's friend, Sukhotin, who simultaneously appropriated it from an extensive book of protocols or lecture notes that he found hidden in an iron chest at Zionist headquarters in France, but also in Alsace and in Switzerland. They were also stolen from Herzl's house in Vienna and the secret vault of the Mizraim lodge. They were delivered to Nilus in 1897 by a Russian spy and equally by Sukhotin in 1901. At the same time, the French translation of a Hebrew original was sent from Paris by Rachkovsky to the Russian interior ministry in 1897 and then delivered to Nilus.

As for the first edition that no man has set eyes upon, it was probably never published or was published simultaneously in 1902 and 1905.

Now we are clear on the subject. And whoever cannot grasp this either cannot think logically or is a lackey in the pay of the Jews.

This is a good place to stop. With such dubious credentials a man would have difficulty getting a job as a street cleaner. On the other hand, the gentlemen Nilus, zur Beek, Jouin, Lambelin, and Co. on the basis of such evidence make bloody charges against fifteen million people (a half million of whom live in Germany). They demand the harshest punishments against them. In this manner they want to deflect the attention of people away from the real causes of their miseries and lead them onto false paths. [With the following episode, Segel shows us where these practices can ultimately lead.]

THE DEADLY EFFECT OF
THE *PROTOCOLS*: POGROMS IN RUSSIA

In 1918 yet another new edition appeared in southern Russia under the title *Zionist Protocols: The Plan of World Conquest by the Jews and Freemasons.* It begins with the following words:

These protocols constitute a plan of world conquest carefully worked out in all particulars by the Jews. The largest part of the program has already been realized, and unless we come to our senses we shall be hopelessly doomed to destruction. . . . These protocols are in fact the key to understanding our first abortive revolution in 1905; they also explain our second revolution of 1917, in which the Jews played so fatal a role for Russia. . . . For those of us who are witnesses to the self-laceration of Russia, for those of us who hope to experience Russia's rebirth, this document is all the more vital because it reveals the means by which the enemies of Christianity enslave us. Once we have gained knowledge of these methods, it will be possible to win the battle against the enemies of Christ and of Christian culture.

This edition was distributed in tens of thousands of copies to the soldiers of the White Army, active against the Bolsheviks in southern Russia in 1920 and under the leadership of generals Denikin, Mamontov, and Wrangel. The Bolsheviks had established their power in the north, in Petrograd and Moscow [following the 1917 revolution]. Although peasants in southern Russia and the Ukraine seized upon the Bolsheviks' slogans, drove out the officials and the nobility, and redistributed the land among themselves, there reigned among them from the outset a strong political and national resentment of the Bolsheviks' centralizing domination. Tsarist counterrevolutionaries exploited the hostility of the southern population to organize a war against Moscow, depicting the revolution and Bolshevism as the work of the Jews. In this way, counterrevolution would appear, not as a struggle against compatriots, but against the Jewish world conspiracy aimed at Russia and the Christian religion. The *Protocols* furnished clear proof of the Jewish conspiracy. To this end the book was massively distributed among the soldiers [of the White Army]. Those who could read were ordered to read the book aloud to those who could not. The *Protocols* had the desired effect. The Jewish massacres of 1918–20 in southern Russia were among the cruelest in history. They numbered at the very least an estimated 120,000 victims. In whole towns the Jewish population was virtually exterminated, their homes plundered and burned.

Nevertheless, the counterrevolution failed utterly. Behind the lines of the White Army there emerged the old noble landowners and a staff of former tsarist officials who began to repossess the land by driving off the peasants. Since 90 percent of the soldiers [in the White Army] were peasants, however, these actions found no favor among them. They ceased being concerned about Jews and Freemasons and the conspiracy against Christianity and went over to the Bolsheviks in masses. Thus this fifth edition of the *Protocols* (1918) achieved only half its purpose of lethal pogroms against Jews.

§

A look into the contents of this strange document will open to the reader a world full of amazing ideas and bizarre conceptions that offend common sense and human reason.

THE DOCTRINES OF THE ELDERS OF ZION

Supposedly, the *Protocols* was divulged by the supreme leader of the Jewish world conspiracy in twenty-four secret sessions during the First Zionist Congress at Basel, in August 1897. The Elders of Zion constitute the central committee of the Zionists and keep guard over the "secrets of the Jews." Periodically, the Elders prescribe policies and actions for the entire Jewish people. The audience addressed by the supreme leader must be thought of as a band of coconspirators that listens silently and in blind obedience. They make no comments and raise no objections.

The twenty-four speeches contain two themes. The speaker reprises all that the Jewish world conspiracy has thus far achieved, the basis for all its activities and their justification. Beyond this, the speaker develops the program for the immediate future. It may be remarked here that the Elders of Zion in the autumn of 1897 speak of the world war and the League of Nations (at least in the German translation of Gottfried zur Beek). This irrefutably proves that the Elders of Zion direct the destiny of Europe. What they decided in 1897 was promptly carried out in 1914 and 1919.

The supreme leader of the Elders of Zion appears to be the most powerful man on the globe. He speaks in a tone and with an authority that surpasses the speeches of the mightiest potentates on earth. Truly admirable is the Jews' ability to veil the institutions of the Elders of Zion in so much mystery that no man in the world has even an inkling of the identity or dwelling place of the leader or his associates. All we know for sure is that the Elders of Zion are closely allied to the Freemasons, who blindly do their bidding.

THE POLITICAL PHILOSOPHY OF THE *PROTOCOLS*
Right from the outset, the speaker begins developing his political philosophy and the moral principles upon which the policies of the Elders of Zion are based:

Men are by nature evil, self-seeking, violence-prone, and ruthless. All men seek power and there is scarcely one who would not be willing to sacrifice the general good for the sake of his personal advantage. In the governance of the state, much more is achieved by ruthless force than by reasonable discussion or moral persuasion. Force alone is decisive. Law is founded on force and power. Political liberty is merely an idea, an abstraction, not a reality. Politics has nought to do with the moral law. The term "right" is a limited, by no means universally valid, concept.

The evil being unleashed will pass; it will lead eventually to a greater and more general welfare. The end justifies the means. Only a singular person, trained to self-mastery from childhood, can fully understand the basic principles and tendencies of our program. It follows from this that the most suitable form of state is the one in which governance lies in the hands of one responsible person. Without this absolute power, morality cannot prosper in the state.

The masses are blind, wholly without reason or judgment. They are barbarians who bring to bear their raw barbarism at every opportunity. Bereft of a king or emperor to lead it, a people destroys itself.

It follows logically from all this that the slogan of the Elders of Zion can only be: Power and Deception. Power is the foundation, but cunning and slyness are the operational means, the only ways to achieve the projected goals. Bribery, fraud, and betrayal are all acceptable as long as they serve the attainment of the goals.

TERROR AS A TOOL OF GOVERNMENT

The Chief Sage of Zion lays out the ethical doctrines that justify the means to an end, but for the time being he tells us only briefly what this goal entails: "Our empire will be founded on peaceful conquest. It will replace the horrors of war with less visible, but more effectual, means of coercion. To compel blind and unconditional obedience, it shall establish the Reign of Terror [zur Beek, pp.72–73]."

Apparently, the Elders are Zionist pacifists, for they seek to establish an empire by means of peaceful conquest. However, in place of war they will introduce something that in the thinking of most people is far more unsettling, namely the Reign of Terror. Assassinations of heads of state and other authorities will arouse such horror in ruling circles that none will dare to oppose the will of the Elders of Zion. Everywhere and at all times that murderous attacks have taken place on tsars, kings, ministers, or generals, the hand of the Jews and Freemasons has been at work. Only these aliens and internationalists would employ such extremist methods.

Through the employment of these means, the Elders of Zion will eventually triumph, subjecting all governments to their supreme rule. Clearly, from time immemorial the Elders of Zion have constituted the chief governing body of the world. The secret of their power is in the Reign of Terror. An Elder of Zion has but to move his little finger for heads of state, their ministers, marshals, and generals to blanch with fear. The Tsar of Russia and all the world's other leaders believe they rule because they command huge armies and navies, conclude alliances, conduct open and secret diplomacy, summon parliaments, dismiss ministers, give speeches, and visit one another. What a tremendous self-delusion!

In a hidden, subterranean cave near Basel sit the "real directors" of world history, those who have the right to think that they hold the destinies of nations in their hands. (These Jews are not, in other words, Galician, Lithuanian, and Romanian schoolteachers, Talmudic scholars, store clerks, preachers, and rabbis who have come together to discuss how best to protect themselves from antisemitism and pogroms.) Apparently, however, there are still one or two governments in the world that do not obey [the Elders of Zion] so unconditionally. So intolerable a resistance, the Elders solemnly swear, will be broken: "We shall triumph and *all* governments shall be subjected to our dominion."

LIBERTY,
EQUALITY, FRATERNITY: A SLOGAN INVENTED BY JEWS
We have seen that the Jews confess to having practiced terror for centuries, but another infamy is theirs as well: "Even in antiquity we caused to reverberate from the ranks of the people: Liberty! Equality! Fraternity!" No base deed is too low for the Jews. We thought, and still think, that this fateful slogan of the French Revolution of 1789 was a creation of the French spirit, one in which the French still take pride. Now the Elders of Zion inform us, quite casually, that the Jews were the authors of this crime. In fact we learn something even more interesting from the mouth of the supreme leader of Zion: the entire French Revolution was the work of the Jews. "Consider the French Revolution," he says, "to which we gave the name *Great*. The secrets of its preparation are fully known to us. It was the work of our hands. In every nook and cranny our secret associations introduced the slogan Liberty, Equality, Fraternity, which drew huge masses to our ranks and carried our banner to

victory. This it was that gave us the opportunity to play our highest trump: the abolition of the nobility's privileges."

In the years 1789–90, under the influence of the famous slogan, the French National Assembly declared the possessions of the crown, clergy, and nobility to be national property. It did away with the nobility's titles and all political–social privileges. The assembly issued "Assignats," paper currency based on the confiscated properties. Quickly the value of the Assignats sank dramatically and peasants were able to buy up the estates and castles of the nobility for a song. [During the nineteenth century, a segment of the peasantry prospered to the point that some even bought patents of nobility, thus forming a new rural aristocracy, which to some degree supplanted the old.]

The *Protocols* would like to make it clear that this whole upheaval was the work of the Jews. In fact, only a handful of Jews were present in France at that time, and they lived in the city (not the countryside). Half of the Jews resided in Alsace-Lorraine and made scanty livings as peddlers and moneylenders. Not a single Jew figured in the buying up of noble estates — they were prohibited from owning farmland. Still less were they the heirs to noble political and social privileges. At the outbreak of the revolution, Jews were not even citizens and became such only on 27 September 1791, after a long, difficult debate in the National Assembly.[24]

Outside France, the great landed aristocrats have retained their privileges to the present day. The emancipation of the peasants in Germany, Austria, and Russia took place years after the French Revolution. Only with the upheaval in Russia [in 1917] was the nobility expropriated in favor of the peasantry, as is generally known. In a somewhat milder form this happened also in Poland, Romania, and Czechoslovakia, where a partial expropriation of the great estates was legislatively accomplished.

THE STRUGGLE
AGAINST THE NOBILITY AND THE GREAT ESTATES
In another passage the Elders of Zion declare: "The non-Jewish nobility has exhausted its political power. We need no longer con-

cern ourselves with this. However, because great landowners exist, enjoy a socially secure position, and often remain wholly independent, they are a danger to us. Therefore, we must rob them of their landed property at any price. The best means of doing this is to raise the land tax and other tax burdens, thus effecting their indebtedness and seeing to it that they overextend themselves."

Here we see the whole measure of Jewish trickery and baseness. First they abolish the political privileges of the nobility, destroying its influence in state affairs. But the nobility retains its lands, which make them independent and therefore threatening to the Jews. At once, the Elders of Zion raise the land tax and other burdens; the nobility falls deeper and deeper into debt; noblemen must sell off their patrimonial estates and take up the beggar's staff.

§

This higher form of absurdity struck a responsive chord in the most educated circles. On 23 April 1924, in the week of the Kant jubilee and on the eve of the Reichstag elections, Professor [Hans] Kania, the historical scholar, gave a lecture in Potsdam concerning the *Protocols*. He held forth about how wonderful it was that this remarkable historical and political document of 1897 had predicted events that were borne out a generation later. It was only logical to assume that those who foresaw these events were the very same people who caused them, that the Elders of Zion therefore constituted the secret supreme government of the world. Among other things, he touched upon the previously mentioned plan to ruin the great landholders through higher taxes. Professor Kania opined that the *Protocols* ought to make an enormous impression on our great landholders. "All this has been predicted. Should the democratic parties take up these demands in the Reichstag, it will become clear to the nobility that the Jews have done this and have thereby brought a part of their plan to fruition."

If ever a bill is proposed to the Reichstag that the agrarian interests find unacceptable, they will immediately realize who is behind it and what their real goal is. The Elders of Zion stand behind it and stand also at the head of the Jewish world conspiracy, which seeks to destroy all Christian states so as to erect its own Jewish-Masonic world empire upon the ruins. In that state the Antichrist himself will govern. How better to begin the destruction of Christian states than to rob, impoverish, and drive the Christian nobility out of public life?

It is obvious what valuable service the *Protocols* can perform for certain political parties. And it is easy to understand why the reactionary forces in their totality cling to the *Protocols* and stubbornly insist upon its authenticity, despite all contrary evidence. Such a weapon — "a full and indisputable confession from the Jews" — is not so easily surrendered.

NAPOLEON III AND THE ELDERS OF ZION

At this point, anyone who is not altogether mentally impaired ought to ask a question. When and where did the Christian nobility lose its political power? Certainly not in Germany or Russia, where up to the most recent period this class has controlled domestic and foreign policy and military force, and where only as an exception has it allowed middle-class people to participate in power. Such participation has been more or less the case only in France, where the feudal nobility was divested of its political power to make room for the bourgeoisie in 1790. There, as we have seen, a great part of the nobility's property was nationalized and sold at ridiculously low prices to the peasantry. The remaining property of the nobility was still large and grew further in the following decades, but despite this the nobility was unable to regain its former predominance in politics.

Nevertheless, anyone who saw the nobility as an enemy would certainly try to strike at it through its wealth. This whole train of thought [in the *Protocols*] points to France. Any knowledgeable person ought to suspect immediately that [the Chief Sage of Zion's lecture] is an echo of a speech made in France, reflecting French conditions. And, in fact, the Emperor Napoleon III waged a battle against the old feudal nobility, which had been regaining some of its former strength. The nobles were by and large legitimists, that is, supporters of the old Bourbon or Orleans dynasties who regarded

Napoleon as a usurper. It was Napoleon who in the late 1840s and 1850s employed the means against the nobility that the Elders of Zion recommended fifty years later![25]

What a highly curious fact. What does Napoleon III have to do with the Elders of Zion?

Other "coincidences" are worth mentioning here. The political philosophy of the Elders of Zion, the moral principles advanced to justify their actions, their attitude toward the great masses of the people, indeed, even the constitution they outline — all these bear a clear Napoleonic stamp. Any reader of the *Protocols* familiar with the history of Napoleon III must say to himself: either Napoleon III was the pupil of the Elders of Zion or vice versa. There certainly exists an unambiguous spiritual affinity between these two powers.

THE BOOK
FROM WHICH THE FORGERS STOLE THEIR WISDOM

[Segel reminds the reader of the discovery made in 1921 by the *Times* of London's Constantinople correspondent, Philip Graves. Further research revealed that this was the book by Maurice Joly, *Dialogue between Machiavelli and Montesquieu in Hell* (1864), a no-holds-barred satire on the reign of Napoleon III.]

Joly's book pilloried Napoleon III, whose pseudodemocratic rule concealed the crassest of tyrannies. To achieve his purposes, he pitted all the parties against one another, muzzled freedom of thought and expression, corrupted the press with utmost cynicism, and shrank before no lie or fraud when it was a matter of manipulating public opinion or covering up some crime. . . .

In the *Protocols*, all the philosophical and moral principles that are put in the mouth of the Chief Sage of Zion come right out of the speeches of Machiavelli-Napoleon in Maurice Joly's satire. They make sense in this French book, as does the plan to raise the land tax in order to undermine the material basis of the nobility. Napoleon III actually did this. The "authors" of the *Protocols* plagiarized mindlessly, calculating that the long-forgotten book by Joly would not be discovered. It was only by chance that it came to light.

When pickpockets are caught in the act, they are never embarrassed. On the spot, they fabricate an alibi to get themselves out of a jam. As mentioned above, the antisemitic forgers made Joly into a Jew by the name of Joel, a precursor of Judeo-Bolshevism and the Elders of Zion.

Even today, as the saying goes, "Lies have short legs." In November 1924 the Paris journal *Paix et Droit* [Peace and law] printed excerpts from Joly's autobiography (1878), part of a collection of autobiographies by famous lawyers housed in the Bar Association Library of Paris. In it, Joly discloses his origins. He was descended from a strictly Catholic family, closely related to the provincial nobility. His father and grandfather were high government officials. He includes his baptismal certificate from the church register with the names of the officiating priest and godmother.

The assertion by Lord Alfred Douglas that Joly was circumcised as Moses Joel, an assertion adopted by all the apostles of the *Protocols* in Germany and repeated with absolute certainty by the Vienna edition of 1925, is demonstrably a brazen, shameless lie.

§

THE JEWS AS WORLD CORRUPTERS
In another passage, the leader of the Elders of Zion states: "There is nothing more dangerous than the power of the personality. Therefore, we must so direct the education of the non-Jewish world that it falls into hopeless weakness when confronted by any matter that requires energy and decisiveness." We have seen how the Elders of Zion ruin the nobility by means of mounting land taxes. Simultaneously, they afford protection to commerce and industry. Thus envy and jealousy between these classes will be even more intensified. But to keep commerce and industry from becoming too great, they foster speculation with all their might, thus creating a counterweight against honest trade. All social classes must be set against one another and thus debilitated. To this end, hate, envy, and discord will be injected among them. The Elders of Zion have

arranged it so that industry drains off money from agriculture and labor; then through speculation all the world's treasure will be delivered up to the Jews. The goyim will be impoverished and will have to bow before the Jews for the sake of eking out the barest of livings.

Just as the Christian nobility was ruined by higher taxes, so the Christian industrialists will be led to their destruction. The Jews will tempt them to make excessive expenditures to support a lordly lifestyle, far out of proportion to their incomes. This will result in physical and moral degeneration in the families of the Christian industrialists. Their progeny will lack the energy to carry on or develop the work of their fathers, which will then fall into Jewish hands.

The most important method by which the Jews undermine Christian industry is the seduction of the labor force into demanding ever higher wages, if need be by fomenting strikes. But higher wages do not benefit labor because Jews have simultaneously raised the prices of basic necessities. The result is mutual class hatred, eternal discord, and general confusion. Just as every rise in the land tax proceeds from the Jews, so, too, every greater or lesser strike is the work of the concealed hand of the Jews. Were there no Jewish agitators, prices would not go higher.

RUSSIAN METHODS

In tsarist Russia, the government customarily shifted blame for every strike onto the Jews, pointing to revolutionaries with Jewish names, even when the strike was economic, not political or revolutionary, in nature. In many cases, the police succeeded in convincing workers that they were merely the tools of the Jews. The lower middle class and peasantry always succumbed to this argument.

On 30 October 1905, Tsar Nicholas II issued the famous "October Manifesto," in which he renounced his rights as an absolute monarch and introduced a constitution and parliament. Thereupon, the head of the reactionary party, Minister of Police D. F. Trépov, unleashed a veritable bloodbath in the Pale of Settlement[26] by telling the peasants that the Jews had coerced the tsar into treading upon the sacred autocracy and that the constitution was the work of the devil, designed to destroy Russia. *We shall see below that the* Protocols *were composed and printed at just about this time.*

The publication and dissemination of the *Protocols* in the German language by certain circles is nothing less than the shameless attempt to transplant these Russian methods of deflection and deception onto German soil. Reactionaries in Germany and throughout the world go hand in hand. Even now, once again, all the progressive movements of the world are being brought into disrepute by portraying them as the machinations of the Jews, as the means by which the Jews achieve world domination.

THE FOREIGN AND DOMESTIC POLICY OF THE ELDERS OF ZION

As we all know, high-level politics breaks down into internal and external policies. The cleverest statesmen are the ones who conduct both according to the same set of principles. This is the way the Elders of Zion proceed, as well. Just as they sow class hatred, dissension, and quarreling at home, so do they in the world at large. Let us listen to their "own" words: "In Europe and through its connections to all quarters of the globe we must incite ferment, conflict, and enmity. As soon as a non-Jewish state dares to offer us resistance, we must be in a position to cause neighboring states to make war on it. But if its neighbors try to make common cause with it and proceed against us, we must then unshackle world war."

THE SECRET OF THE WORLD WAR

In these lines is revealed the great and ghastly secret of who it was that started the war of 1914–18. Democratic and socialist journalists, politicians, professors, and parliamentarians — all corrupted by the Jews — indict one or another head of state, ambassador, minister, general, and the like. Swindle! Now we know better. There it is in black and white: at the end of August 1897, the Elders of Zion, gathered in Basel, took the irrevocable decision for war. From that day they quietly prepared the war behind the backs of the statesmen. In the August days of 1914, the Elders of Zion gave the high sign to the Russian, German, and French general staffs, and armies mobilized. World war was a finished deal. Generals and ministers never suspected whose orders they were really obeying. That's how skillfully the Jews concealed the fact that it was they who set the world ablaze.

That the world war actually happened is, of course, yet another proof of the authenticity of the *Protocols,* which foretells it all.

"Good Lord! What horrifying power these confounded Jews possess," say the millions of educated and half-educated when they read the lines from the *Protocols* quoted here. If a state dares to defend itself, then its neighbors fall upon it. But if all countries rise up against them, then the Jews pull a world war out of their sleeves, as we experienced all too frightfully in 1914. Professor Kania remarks, apropos of all this, and with the dispassion of the conscientious researcher: "If one reads [the quoted lines] objectively, one can espy the prophecy of the world war."

Needless to say, all this is lifted from Joly's book and appropriately adapted. Napoleon III met every domestic disturbance by provoking class struggle at home; he preempted a threatened revolution by recourse to foreign wars. Other absolute monarchs behaved similarly. The tsar's camarilla, it will be recalled, caused the war with Japan only in the hope that an imminent revolution could be avoided.[27] After the loss of the war the revolution broke out anyway.

On page 58 of [Joly's book], Machiavelli-Napoleon speaks about this to Montesquieu: "Absolutist governments must be in a position to react to every internal disturbance with a civil war, and to every imminent revolution with a general war, a universal war." "Napoleon III" preaches what he, in fact, practiced. To be sure, in Joly's book Napoleon does not speak of world war but of general war (in French, *guerre universelle,* not *guerre mondiale*). Similarly, Nilus writes in the Russian edition not of world war (*mirovaia voina*) but of general war (*vseobshchaia voina*).

In olden times there was a saying among thieves: He who steals stolen goods shall not be held accountable. Neither in 1864, when Joly wrote, nor in 1905, when Nilus plagiarized him, was the concept of *world war* in use. Gottfried zur Beek was the first to inject this falsehood into the *Protocols* [in 1919]. It was by this and other falsifications of Nilus — together making for one grand falsification — that zur Beek and the other translators premeditatedly spread the belief throughout the world that the *Protocols* was discussing the World War of 1914–18.

THE LEAGUE OF NATIONS — A WORK OF THE JEWS
Neither Joly nor Nilus could even conceive of a world war, and it would have been just as unnatural for them to have thought of a League of Nations.[28] In zur Beek's translation, however, the league is center stage. It is the task of the Jewish-Freemason lodges, according to zur Beek, to convince the nations that the goal [of the league] is the general welfare of peoples, brotherhood, and equality. In reality, its purpose is the world domination of the Jews. "Naturally, the nations will not be told that this league will be formed under our sole control."

"That's it!" shouts the gullible philistine. "The hateful League of Nations is nothing more than a Jewish enterprise. The Elders of Zion decreed the League in 1897, and a generation later it came to pass. Yet another proof for the authenticity of the *Protocols!*"

However, "honest" Nilus does not use the Russian for League of Nations, but simply refers to an *association*. This colorless word would make not the slightest impression [on zur Beek's readers]. *League of Nations,* on the other hand, opens broad new vistas, affords a glimpse into the deepest secrets of world politics, and awakens a storm of emotion in the breast of every German superpatriot. When the Jews assure us that this League of Nations can come into being only because they control it, then everyone will know what to think of this creation.

THE CARELESS FORGERS
"The liar must have a good memory," goes the old adage. If a liar or forger gets careless, he can easily be unmasked. So it happened, and more than once, with our protocol fabricators. Here is one example. The Elders of Zion decree the following: "To gain our desired end [the total ruin of non-Jewish Europe], we shall take care to have

elected presidents whose pasts are blemished, as with the case of the Panama scandal."²⁹ This decision was supposedly made in August 1897. It corresponds to actual events when a president was elected [in France] who was connected to the Panama scandal. This person could only be Emile Loubet, who became president of the French Republic on 18 February 1899. Obviously, then, these lines [from the *Protocols*] could not have been written in August 1897. The events of those distant days had become confused in the forgers' minds.

And here is another slip. In August 1897 the Elders of Zion speak of one of their French confidants and commissars, the Freemason Leon Bourgeois, as coming out in favor of progressive methods of instruction. The Elders of Zion, as we know, are archreactionaries and antidemocrats and therefore they hate all modern institutions, including progressive education. Leon Bourgeois advocated these educational methods, it goes without saying, on orders from the Jews and Freemasons, so that Christians would be made more stupid and all the easier to deliver into the hands of the Jewish world conspiracy. Remember, this was all discussed by the Elders in Basel in August 1897. However, let us pick up the official program for French public schools (1922–23). There we can read the original decree of Minister of Education Leon Bourgeois concerning progressive methods of instruction. It is dated 17 and 20 December 1898, therefore sixteen months later than when the forgers of the *Protocols* have it being discussed by the Elders of Zion. Clearly, these lines from the *Protocols* could only have been written after December 1898. Once again, the forgers were "unlucky" in their choice of dates.

THE ULTRAREACTIONARY ELDERS OF ZION
The examples here reveal the Elders' political attitudes. Astonishingly, when it comes to the masses, democracy, rights of the people, and institutions of the modern state, this society of Jews and Freemasons *thinks exactly like the tsar and his most reactionary servants*. We cannot, therefore, imagine why these people would want to destroy the tsarist system instead of enlisting it to strengthen their domi-

nance over the masses. In many respects the Elders are more exacting than the bloodiest of tsars.

THEIR HARSHNESS TOWARD FORMER ALLIES

The archconspirators, engaged in subterranean plots, promise:

Once we have attained full mastery, we will know how to prevent any sort of conspiracies against us. Anyone who takes up weapons against our rule will be mercilessly executed. Anyone who aids or abets a secret society will also be punished with death. All existing secret societies, about which we are fully informed and which have rendered and continue to render us valuable service, shall be dissolved. Their members shall be exiled from Europe. So, too, shall we deal with all the non-Jewish Freemasons who have penetrated too deeply into our secrets. We shall issue an edict by which all former members of secret societies shall be banished from Europe, the headquarters of our government.

These sentences are enough to send shivers up the spine. The philistine casts his eyes to the heavens and thinks to himself: "Such cruelty, such malice is unprecedented!" The Jewish masters of the world are the first to have sunk so low. Flushed with their brutal triumph, the Jews know no bounds.

But whoever is familiar with the history of the nineteenth century will recall immediately that Napoleon III, following his coup d'état of 2 December 1851, behaved exactly as the Elders of Zion planned in August 1897 in order to establish their Jewish-Masonic world empire. Immediately upon making himself the ruler of the French, Napoleon was faced with armed resistance to his domination. He mercilessly executed countless insurgents. At least twenty-six thousand members of the secret societies that had rendered him good service up to the point of his coup were banned to French penal colonies in Africa and South America. Did the French usurper have a presentiment about the plans of the Elders of Zion — a half century before they were made?

THEIR HOSTILITY TOWARD PUBLIC EDUCATION

The Elders of Zion plan to establish a government compared to which the government of Tsar Nicholas I would seem mild, in fact, highly liberal. Needless to say, there will be no parliaments in this empire. The Elders of Zion have developed a sophisticated system for hobbling and corrupting the press, combining all the features of Russian and Napoleonic censorship. They will tailor the public school system to avoid education at any price, for nothing is more dangerous to the welfare of the state than educated people. Universities will be crippled and academic freedom abolished. Professors will regard themselves as state functionaries and teach only what the state prescribes. They will banish from their curricula anything to do with politics, for politics spoils the character of the young, makes them rebellious, and inclines them to disobey government injunctions. "Unconditional obedience to authority will be the chief trait of our legislation."

This ought to suffice to show the reader what spirit animates the Elders of Zion and what kind of order they will impose on the state they intend to establish.

THE JEWS
PLAN TO BLOW UP THE WHOLE NON-JEWISH WORLD

We have seen what horrifying and destructive plans the Jewish world conspiracy has in store for the Christian peoples. In this context, the Chief Sage of Zion remarks to his audience:

You might well object that, when the non-Jews finally figure out how everything we do fits together, they will be so embittered as to take up weapons against us. For this eventuality we reserve the ultimate weapon, before which even the bravest will quail. Soon all the world's major cities will be crisscrossed with subway tunnels.[30] Should we be endangered, we shall by means of these tunnels blow whole cities to kingdom come, including state offices, archives, and the non-Jews with all their possessions!

Amazingly, this is a direct quotation from a book read and fervently believed by millions of Germans in the twentieth century. It is incomprehensible that this passage, by itself, has not sufficed to consign the entire book to the realm of the absurd or to make the public influence of its distributors forever impossible. . . .

Unfortunately, the Elders of Zion do not tell us what steps they are taking to prevent this catastrophe from engulfing the Jews as well. Otto Friedrich aptly describes this "plan" as the fantasy of a police spy. But it is worth noting that even the most imaginative police spy could not have come up with this horror story in 1896 or 1897. Nobody would then have foreseen that "soon all the major cities will be crisscrossed with subway tunnels." Perhaps, six or seven years later, after the opening of the Berlin system (1903), optimists might hypothesize that the world's other major cities would follow suit. But even today this is not yet true.

[Theodor] Fritsch, publisher of a [German] translation of the *Protocols,* seems to have some doubts about this passage. He comments: "This idea is so insane that the healthy mind rebels against its credibility. Surely the speaker [in the *Protocols*] only wanted to make it understood that the conspiracy would shrink from no means, however wicked, to carry out its intentions. The sinking of [the ship carrying] Lord Kitchener and his staff by the infernal machines of the Jews, as described by reliable sources in no. 509 of the *Hammer,* is an instructive example of what the Jewish conspiracy is capable of."

From these lines we learn incidentally that the commander in chief of the English army, Lord Kitchener, whose staff ship hit a mine and sank on the high seas, was also a victim of the Elders of Zion. Thus, with one hand the Jews sank the English flagship, and with the other they stabbed the German army in the back.[31] Quite an achievement! These Jewish "infernal machines" ought to be patented. Most of the other translations of the *Protocols* do not even consider an explanation of these points necessary; they are confident that their readers will accept this hoax, too.

§

Readers ought now to be familiar enough with the contents and the thought processes of the *Protocols of the Elders of Zion.* We can now proceed to show the sources that produced this monument of "noble spirit," a monument that for six or seven years has won the gullible admiration of "educated" Germans.

As mentioned earlier, a few months after Gottfried zur Beek's German edition of the *Protocols*, Dr. J. Stanjek pointed to the striking similarity between its plan of Jewish world conquest and that developed by the pulp fiction writer Hermann Goedsche in his 1868 novel, *Biarritz*. The plan of world conquest in the *Protocols* can also be found in compressed form in the "rabbi's speech concerning the goyim," delivered, according to the novel, in secret to a meeting of Jews. Zur Beek printed this "rabbi's speech," a capsule version of the *Protocols,* to prove that the Jewish plans of world conquest had existed for ages. It will be recalled that Otto Friedrich took the trouble to compare the two documents minutely and was able to show that the two plans of world conquest were nearly identical in their structure and main lines of thought. Even the words used are very nearly the same. We quote now from Friedrich's book:[32]

RABBI'S SPEECH	GOEDSCHE
The stock exchange regulates and keeps track of the debts of states, and we are in most places the masters of the stock exchange. We must endeavor, therefore, to make it easier for [the states] to contract debts, so we can control prices. As collateral for the credit we extend to countries, we must take their railroads, mines, forests, smelting works, and factories. (zur Beek, p.32)	Because we control the stock exchange, we control the wealth of states. Therefore, we must make it easier for states to contract debts, so as to gain ever greater control of them. Wherever possible, capital must take as collateral state institutions, railroads, revenues, mines, entitlements, domains. (*Biarritz,* p.173)
Agriculture will always constitute the greatest wealth of a country. Great landowners will always command respect and influence. It follows that we must make it our aim for our brothers in Israel to gain control of the large estates. Under	Landed property will always be the iron and indestructible wealth of a country. In and of itself it affords power, influence, and respect. Therefore, landed property must be transferred into the hand of Israel. . . . Under the pretense that we

the pretext that we are helping the working classes, we must shift the entire tax burden onto the great estate owners. When their estates fall to us, the labor of the Christian proletariat will be of immense profit to us. (zur Beek, p.32)

want to protect labor and ease the lot of the poorer classes, we must put the whole burden of state and communal taxes on landed property. If agricultural land is in our hands, then the labor of Christian farmers and workers will yield us profits tenfold. (*Biarritz*, p.174)

Every war, every revolution, every political and religious alteration brings us ever closer to attainment of our highest goal. (zur Beek, p.32)

The instability of thrones lets our power and influence grow. To this end, we see to continuing unrest. Every revolution yields interest for our capital and takes us forward to our goal. (*Biarritz*, p.178)

Commerce and speculation, two rich sources of our profit, we may never allow to be snatched from the hands of Israelites. Above all, we must protect our trade in alcohol, butter, bread, and wine because in this way we become the absolute lords of agriculture. (zur Beek, pp.32–33)

All trade that involves speculation and earnings must be in our hands. Above all, we must own the trade in liquor, oil, wool, and grain because then we will control agriculture and the land. (*Biarritz*, p.180)

These small samples should suffice to demonstrate that the "rabbi's speech" of Gottfried zur Beek is nothing other than the intellectual product of the departed Hermann Goedsche. We have already spoken of this "man of honor." In *Biarritz* (1868), the chapter entitled "In the Jewish Cemetery of Prague" (pp.191–93) tells how, according to Goedsche's fantasies, every hundred years the princes of the twelve tribes of Israel gather in the ancient, legendary Prague cemetery. There they report to each other about how far they have progressed toward world mastery and then hatch plans for the next hundred years. On the last day of the Feast of Tabernacles the hundred years is up, and on the eve of this day the prescribed assembly takes place—spied upon by a converted Jew and a Christian. ("A cold shudder went up their spines; their hearts trembled with the horror.") With the help of a lot of gothic details, Goedsche describes how the unearthly shapes of the Jewish tribal leaders slink in from all directions to be greeted by their chief. Then each of the twelve recounts how many millions reside in the Jewish banks of his city, whereupon are laid out the plans for the future (a few fragments of which we have just examined).

Comically, Goedsche's account has the heads of the *twelve* tribes of Israel assemble. But every schoolboy knows from Biblical history that King Sargon of Assyria led the *ten* tribes of Israel into exile in 722 B.C., whereupon they vanished. The Jews living in Europe today are the descendants of only *two* tribes. Great minds cannot attend to such details, however.

WHO WAS SIR JOHN RETCLIFFE?

From the foregoing it is clear that all the essentials of the cemetery scene reappear in the rabbi's speech cited by zur Beek as proof of a Jewish world conspiracy, as described in the *Protocols*. This supports the suspicion that Goedsche was also the author of the rabbi's speech that has been the main showpiece among antisemitic propagandists since 1901 (although it originated much earlier). The French translator of the *Protocols,* Monsignor Jouin, utilizes the rabbi's speech for the same purposes as zur Beek but also tells us something interesting about its origins: an Englishman named Sir John Retcliffe published it in the French journal *Le Contemporain* [The contemporary] in 1886. Apparently, Msgr. Jouin did not know that Sir John Retcliffe was the pseudonym for Hermann Goedsche. Thus, eighteen years after writing the cemetery scene of 1868, Goedsche reworked it into the rabbi's speech. And this rabbi's speech as used by Gottfried zur Beek must now stand witness to what? The veracity of the *Protocols*? Or perhaps just the cemetery scene from the novel?

The intellectual gem of the night scene in the cemetery at Prague was probably published soon as a piece separate from the novel. It appeared in Russian translation in 1872 and has served since as a preparatory tool for pogroms. In 1903 the organizers of the gruesome pogrom at Kishinev, Bessarabia, reissued the book [describing the meeting at Prague] and circulated it massively among the common people.[33] The *Protocols of the Elders of Zion* has made it popular once again. In Germany following the revolution [of 1918], it celebrated a double resurrection. Karl Rohm (of Lorch, Württemberg) published it under the title *Was ist jüdischer Geist?* [What is the Jewish spirit?]. Its preface states:

Decades ago the writer John Retcliffe saw through the international politics of world Jewry and published the facts known to him in the form of an historical novel. But the Hebrews bought up all the copies of the book and prevented its republication. Today, it is no longer possible to obtain the book in which the following midnight scene in the Jewish cemetery at Prague is described. Because Judah has today (1919) all but achieved its hidden goals, John Retcliffe's warning to the whole non-Jewish world, even though it may be fifty or sixty years old, is still of sufficient interest to be newly submitted to the German people.

The notorious Berlin newspaper publisher "Blackjack" Kunze came out in 1919 with a new edition [of the cemetery scene] entitled: *The Secret of Jewish World Dominance: From a Work of the Previous Century Which Vanished from the Book Trade Because the Jews Bought It Up.*[34] The foreword says: "There is nothing, we are convinced, that can preach so effectively to the masses of our erring people concerning the dreadful power and brutality of Jewry as John Retcliffe's chapter on the Jewish cemetery in Prague. . . . "

THE NOBLE GOEDSCHE'S WORK

It is informative to see what the promulgators of the *Protocols* say in response to the findings of a Stanjek or Friedrich. They portray Goedsche, the scandal-mongering writer of trashy novels, as a serious investigator, a knowing prophet, who was initiated into the conspiratorial plans of the Jews by no less a one than — and this is truly shameless — Ferdinand Lassalle. None other than Lassalle was supposedly the "converted Jew" who along with Goedsche spied upon the secret assembly of Jewish tribal leaders in the Prague cemetery. (Incidentally, Lassalle was not a convert.) Lassalle, actually one of the Elders of Zion preparing the world revolution, had conducted all his agitation on behalf of the working class simply to undermine the Christian states and to establish the rule of the Jews upon their ruins.

In this way a manifest plagiarism [of Goedsche's novel] was fashioned into a proof of the authenticity of the *Protocols* and the existence of a Jewish world conspiracy.

§

THE SECOND
SOURCE OF THE *PROTOCOLS*: JOLY'S DIALOGUE
Earlier we saw by means of a few examples how the fabricators of the *Protocols* plundered the book of the Frenchman Maurice Joly. Now we shall compare a series of passages from the *Protocols* with the appropriate ones from Joly's book so that the reader may gain deeper insight into the plagiarists' work.

ZUR BEEK

I maintain that men of evil instinct are more numerous than those of good character. [Therefore,] far more will be achieved in the state through force and unscrupulousness than through rational discussion. Every man strives after power; every man wants to be his own decision maker and to dictate to others whenever possible. This will to power is so strong that there is scarcely a man who would not be ready to sacrifice the general welfare for the sake of his own advantage. What basic instinct rules the beast of prey we call man? What has guided

JOLY

Evil instincts among men are much stronger than the good. Men are more strongly drawn by evil than by good. Fear and power dominate him better than reason. All men strive for domination. All men would be oppressors if they but could. All of them, or almost all, are ready to sacrifice the rights of others to their own interests. . . . What binds together the beasts of prey called men? When human society first arose, it was raw, unregulated power. Later it was the law, that is, once again, power, now fixed in form. Consult any historical source all his actions and desires throughout all time? When human society arose, men subjected themselves first to raw, blind power, then to law, which is this same power in veiled form. Therefore, I conclude that power alone is decisive. From this, it follows: the basic law of existence rests wholly on the idea that might makes right. Political liberty is an idea, an abstraction, but it is not a fact. . . . (zur Beek, p.68)

Our slogan is Power and Cunning. Power is the foundation, but cunning and subtlety are its tools. These means are the only suitable ones to attain the end that hovers before us. Thus we do not shrink from corruption, fraud, and treason should they serve our purposes. To compel absolute, blind obedience, our empire must erect the Reign of Terror. (zur Beek, pp.72–73)

The word *liberty* plunges human society into a struggle against all powers, against every divine and natural part of the world order. As soon as we sit upon the throne, we shall strike this word from the vocabulary of mankind because it is at the heart

and you will find that everywhere power appeared before law. Political liberty is only a relative term. Necessity rules the states as it does individuals. (Joly, pp.6–7)

Montesquieu: You know only two words: power and cunning. If you raise power to a principle and cunning to the basis for government, then the code of tyranny is no better than that of wild beasts. . . . You think it right to commit treason if it is useful, to kill if it is necessary, to expropriate property if it is advantageous, to misuse public funds, bribe, punish, murder. . . . Machiavelli: But did not you yourself say that the rule of terror was necessary in despotic states, that blind obedience was a necessity to them? (Joly, pp.12–13)

Government by the people destroys all stability and sanctifies an undefined right of revolution. It plunges society into an open battle against all the powers of the divine and human world order. It transforms the people into a beast of prey that is

of that bestial power which reduces the masses to the level of the beast of prey. Only after they have tasted blood are they satisfied. (zur Beek, p.83)	not satisfied until it has tasted blood. (Joly, p.35)
What sort of constitution should we give such a thoroughly corrupted society? . . . Such a society must have a constitution resting on power alone. . . . (zur Beek, p.83)	What sort of constitution do you deem appropriate to such a thoroughly corrupted society? The salvation for such a society, in my opinion, will be the most extreme centralization, that which puts the entire power of the state in the hands of its rulers. (Joly, p.37)
Like the Indian pagan god Vishnu, they will have one hundred hands, and in each shall beat the pulse of a different intellectual tendency. (zur Beek, p.104)	[Machiavelli:] Like the god Vishnu, my press will have a hundred arms, each hand of which will feel all the nuances of public opinion. (Joly, p.106)
Like the pagan god Vishnu with his hundred arms, we shall also have countless resources at our disposal. (zur Beek, p.123)	[Montesquieu:] Now I understand the word of the god Vishnu. You have a hundred arms, like the Indian deity, and each of your fingers touches a spring. (Joly, p.153)
[The Roman general] Sulla cared not a whit for bleeding Italy even though he had taken upon himself guilt for enormous bloodshed. . . . (zur Beek, p.111)	[Machiavelli:] After Sulla had bathed all Italy in blood, he could appear in Rome as a simple citizen, and no one dared to harm a hair on his head. . . . (Joly, p.119)

These examples ought to suffice to illuminate the methods of the plagiarists and falsifiers.[35] They pick out the passages that Joly used to characterize the government and principles of Napoleon III (spoken by Machiavelli) and, after making slight changes, attribute them to the imaginary Elders of Zion. Often, they do so quite clumsily.

§

It often happens that a loose button left at the scene of a crime has betrayed the criminal. The forgers of the *Protocols* have carelessly left a great many such "buttons" lying about. [Segel reiterates how the fabricators of the *Protocols* got their dates mixed up in the case of the "Panama scandal" and Leon Bourgeois's statements concerning progressive education. Now he turns to the more flagrant examples of their self-incrimination.]

Case no.1
On page 139 of zur Beek's book we find the beginning of a long series of tirades describing the tasks of the coming Jewish world ruler and how he will make order out of the present chaos:

Non-Jewish governments find it difficult to stay in power. They are surrounded by societies that we have so thoroughly demoralized that they have lost all faith in God; from out of their midst rise the flames of permanent revolution. The world ruler must dissolve the existing governments and swiftly extinguish this all-consuming fire. It is his duty to liquidate such societies even if it means drowning them in their own blood. . . . The sovereign by divine right has the task of breaking the forces of blind revolution, which partake more of bestial instinct than they do of reason. Under the guise of law and freedom, these forces are now celebrating their triumph with all sorts of robbery and violence. They have destroyed the social order.

At first reading, this passage leaves us dumbfounded. We know without doubt that no single word of it describes European conditions in the 1890s and certainly not those existing in Russia. In the autumn of 1897 the world was quite peaceful. Revolutionary forces slumbered in the depths of the underworld; they did not "celebrate their triumph by committing violence and robbery under the guise of law and freedom." The social order stood firm and was not even thinking about going to rack and ruin. At that time, President

[Félix] Fauré of France made a state visit to the tsar at St. Petersburg. Everywhere splendid celebrations were staged. The two nations pledged brotherly loyalty again and again. Then the tsar visited the capital of his Polish kingdom and stayed there for several days of tumultuous festivities.

On the other hand, the passage does describe literally and exactly the period of the Revolution of 1905 in Russia, following the defeat by Japan. *Then* revolution stormed throughout Russia. The flames of upheaval leapt forth continually in all quarters. *Then* the "blind forces of revolution," guided by bestial instinct rather than human reason, celebrated their triumph with all sorts of violence and robbery committed under the guise of law and liberty. . . . *Then* all social order was destroyed.

This is the way the tsar's courtiers must have seen the events of those days. And the "sovereign by divine right" did, in fact, "liquidate this [revolutionary movement], drowning it in its own blood." He doused the fire of revolution with an ocean of blood. The current president of the Czechoslovak Republic, Tomas Masaryk, recorded Nicholas II as saying: "I would rather cover Russia with crosses than allow the sacred principle of autocracy to be shaken."

Let the reader now decide whether the description of revolutionary conditions was written in 1897 or 1905.

Case no.2
As is well known, Count [Sergei] Witte and his adherents — vilified by their enemies as Jews and Freemasons — succeeded in wresting from Nicholas II the famous October Manifesto (30 October 1905). Under the pressure of events, the "autocrat of all the Russias" voluntarily limited his own powers and bestowed upon his dear people a constitution with a parliament. From that day forth, the traditional absolutism of the Russian tsar ceased to exist.

Strange, in this respect, is the Fifteenth Protocol (p.111 of zur Beek). In it there is a long disquisition on the nature of governmental power. What a blessing it is when the government possesses the unshakable sense of absolute power, which it needs to carry out its functions. Of course, such a sense exists only when the sources of power originate in mysterious attributes, such as selection by God or anointment by the Holy Spirit. "Such absolute power (according to the Fifteenth Protocol, p.111 of zur Beek) the Russian tsar disposed over until quite recently."

But we know that the tsar disposed of such power only until 30 October 1905. Who in his right senses, then, can doubt that this passage was written after that date?

Case no.3

Another passage in the *Protocols* (p.122) asserts: "Freedom of conscience is now universally recognized. Therefore, we can be certain that a few years from now the Christian outlook will completely collapse." But consider the following. Until December 1904, article 196 of the Russian penal code was in force; it stipulated that any deviation from the Orthodox faith was to be punished by banishment to Siberia and the loss of all rights. Only with the edicts of 25 December 1904 and 30 April 1905 was freedom of conscience gradually and partially introduced. Compulsory membership in the Orthodox Church, although slightly modified, remained in force. Before 30 April 1905, there was no freedom of conscience. No reasonable man will doubt that this passage, too, was written after this date.

Case no.4

The last few sessions of the Elders of Zion devote themselves to the operating regulations of the future dynasty of world rulers. Among these, one in particular merits our special attention:

Frequently it will be necessary to deny succession to direct descendants of the king. Lack of seriousness during apprenticeship, effeminacy, or other character traits not only reveal a personal incapacity for government but must severely damage the prestige of authority. Our Elders shall entrust the reins of government only to those who are absolutely qualified to rule firmly and energetically, even to the point where there is danger of cruelty. As soon as the king's will weakens or other signs of incapacity come to light, he will be legally obliged to put the reins of government into more determined hands.

These few sentences are most enigmatic. Even as the Elders of Zion are planning to establish a world empire, they already foresee the possibility that one of the heirs of the dynasty will not be up to the demands of world rule. In truth, among all the riddles cast up by the *Protocols,* this is the most puzzling, although the objective reader can detect an oblique reference to a very real problem here.

Enlightenment can be had by referring to the Soviet government publication in 1918 of documents relating to the prehistory of the October Manifesto, extracted from the tsar by Witte and the liberals. As mentioned above, Witte's opponent was General Trépov. The struggles that preceded the issuing of the manifesto are still not known precisely. But from the Soviet publications it is clear that on the evening of 28 October 1905, Nicholas II, on the urging of Trépov, signed an abdication document in favor of his younger brother, Michael; he was deemed far more energetic than the tsar by Witte's enemies and more likely to deal with the revolution without making concessions. On the next day typesetting of this extensive document was begun in the state printing works. But suddenly the tsar suspended the printing and the finished pages were sent to the state archives (where the Soviet government found and then published them). The wavering tsar had given into liberal pressure, and on 30 October 1905 the manifesto was issued.

The passage from the *Protocols* cited above echoes this abdication episode. Thus, these sentences must have been written after the events described, that is, after 30 October 1905.

What these citations from the text of the *Protocols* demonstrate beyond all doubt is that the present version of the book could not have existed before the autumn of 1905.

§

But these few passages are also well suited to enlighten us on the meaning and purpose of the *Protocols of the Elders of Zion.* They read like a plain warning—really more of a threat—to the heir to the throne of a ruling autocrat who, because of effeminacy and weakness, shows himself incapable of ruling energetically and firmly, "even to the point of cruelty." He is told that in the world empire of the Jews his counterpart would be obliged "to put the reins of government into more energetic hands." That's how the Elders of Zion would treat the sovereign in their empire. How much more was it the duty of the "Elders of St. Petersburg" to replace an enfeebled ruler with one more suited to rule firmly and energetically.

The reader has learned many of the political and governmental principles of the Elders of Zion. These principles surpass in severity the absolutism of any "tsar of all the Russias" and could serve well as models for the "God-anointed" successor of Ivan the Terrible and Nicholas I. The *Protocols* was also well designed to give Tsar Nicholas II "deep insight" into the intrigues and conspiracies of the various political parties vying for dominance in his empire. At the time [of the fabrication of the *Protocols*] the minister of finance, Count Witte, had gained a dangerous influence over the weak-willed and conceited autocrat. Witte was the acknowledged head of a large group of counts, dukes — even a few very wealthy grand dukes — and big industrialists, all of whom cherished a certain liberalism and favored the introduction of constitutional rule on the Western model.

By reading the *Protocols,* however, Nicholas could learn who and what lay behind these liberals: they were tools of the Freemasons, who in turn were the blind instrument of the Jews. These Jews, shrouded in the most mysterious darkness, formed a worldwide association of conspirators, which for centuries had plotted to foment a world revolution, annihilate Christian civilization in its totality, and erect their own empire upon the ruins. By means of unimaginable crimes and shrinking from no atrocity, they strove to achieve this aim. In all of these crimes, liberals such as Witte and his accomplices were deeply implicated. All the assassinations of princes and crimes against the state perpetrated in Russia were nothing more than the work of the "concealed hand" of the Masonic-Jewish alliance. The *Protocols of the Elders of Zion* recorded the general confession of this ruthless secret society, and the document was irrefutably, unimpeachably true.

There was but one means to combat this society: "to drown it in its own blood." This was the meaning of the *Protocols of the Elders of Zion* in its present version, as it was composed of older, some very old, materials and set down finally during the storm of the 1905 revolution and counterrevolution. *The forgers and plagiarists had in mind only one reader — Nicholas II.*

RASPUTIN

The forgers apparently had quite a low opinion of the tsar's political intelligence and critical judgment, for they thought he could be made to swallow the *Protocols* and adjust his policies accordingly. They were correct. The tsar, tsaritsa, a large part of court society, and the highest circles of the nobility and bureaucracy were at that time deeply enmeshed in a web of superstition.

The Rasputin episode is generally known. It began a few years after the appearance of the *Protocols* and came to a bloody end with his murder during the world war. This crafty, illiterate Siberian peasant managed to surround himself with the mystic aura of the religious enthusiast and miracle worker. On the strength of his brutal sensuality and imposing voice, he exercised a fascination upon the ladies of the highest circles in St. Petersburg. They held fast to him and believed in his miraculous powers despite his repeated involvement in scandalous love affairs. The tsaritsa was convinced that he alone could save her sickly son, that only his prayers and laying on of hands had spared the boy from certain death during his attacks.[36]

The royal pair deified the adventurer. Rasputin was able to exert considerable influence on the tsar's most important political and military decisions. Old and trusted state officials and generals, even sitting ministers of state, were dismissed without warning as soon as they earned the displeasure of the all-powerful mystic and magician. In the wartime correspondence between the tsar and his wife, published after the revolution [of 1917], there is a letter from the tsaritsa to her husband at military headquarters in which she implores him to make no important military or political decision without first combing his hair with the enclosed comb of the holy Rasputin.

Small wonder then that the reactionaries at court hoped Nicholas would believe and act upon the fairy tales contained in the *Protocols*.

THE MYSTICAL BACKGROUND OF THE *PROTOCOLS*

The mysticism of the *Protocols* must have appeared far different to the people at court than it would to us. The reader who learns of the *Protocols* in the German or another non-Russian version confronts a long series of banal, mundane lectures delivered by an unknown man to an unknown audience. It seems as though the *Protocols* fell from heaven, and the paltry explanations and inadequate introductions of the translators yield little to the understanding. In the Russian edition, on the other hand, the *Protocols* forms an organic part of a strange book, *The Great in the Small, or the Advent of the Antichrist and the Approaching Rule of the Devil on Earth*. Nilus published this book in Moscow in 1901 without the *Protocols*. As the title indicates, the book is full of mysticism and presents an eccentric theory of the past and future of the human race.

As far as feasible within the present study, we ought to familiarize ourselves with the contents of this book.

§

THE ANTICHRIST BEFORE THE GATES OF ST. PETERSBURG

In 1901, according to Nilus, the Antichrist stood before the gates of St. Petersburg, and the end of the world was nigh. At any moment he might break into holy Russia and make it his own. [Having overcome this last] obstacle, he would complete his domination over the other Christian peoples and establish the devil's rule on earth. Long ago he had overpowered and defeated the rest of Europe, introducing liberal institutions such as constitutions, parliaments, universal suffrage, compulsory education, trial by jury, and so forth. Thus these lands had long ago fallen to the power of the Antichrist and could offer no further resistance to the devil's rule. Luckily, the holy autocracy of the God-anointed tsar still survived in Russia. But as soon as this last dam of the divinely sanctioned world order was breached, the devil's power would flood into the world like a raging river into an unprotected valley. Then there would be no salvation for Christianity, Christian civilization, and Christian peoples.

The theory of the approaching Antichrist is nothing new. Pious theologians in the past have often prophesied it. But Nilus deviates from all his predecessors in the earthly appearance he ascribes to the Antichrist. For example, several centuries ago St. Ephraim preached that the Antichrist would come in the shape of a serpent. The world would be overtaken by horrible events. Hunger, misery, and plagues would rage. The serpent would stamp the mark of its evil on every man's brow and on his right hand, and none would be able to make the sign of the cross. Fearsome and cruel watchmen would let only those with the serpent's mark buy provisions so that the good and the pure would starve. The evil serpent would seek to mimic the Savior in all things, even the virgin birth—but a violated virgin. Aided by a host of demons, the serpent would also mock the miracles of the Savior; he would make seeing men blind. He would lay waste to the churches. There would be no divine service, no mass. After the period of affliction and suffering ran its course, the Lord would come like lightning from the heavens, as it has been promised. Christ would appear in incomparable glory surrounded by the splendor of angelic hosts to pass judgment upon the sinners who had accepted the mark of the serpent, condemning them to eternal damnation in the inextinguishable fires of Hell. But all those who had hidden in caves and forests and spurned the serpent's mark would rejoice with the Bridegroom in heavenly palaces and in the company of the saints forever and ever.

Thus spake St. Ephraim centuries ago. But the holy Nilus is a modern man. His doctrine has a wholly different ring.

According to Nilus, the Antichrist will be an ordinary mortal of Jewish descent. At his appearance all Jews will recognize and hail him as the messiah. With the help of secret societies he will dethrone kings and emperors and establish a mighty empire. His major weapon will be the spread of liberalism and the introduction of its institutions to undermine states and lead them to their ultimate destruction.

Listen to Nilus's own words: "Before the return of the Lord and the Last Judgment will come the other in His name, the Antichrist, who, springing from Jewish blood, will be tsar and master of the whole earth, a messiah out of the House of David, that is, Israel, which bears the guilt for the blood of the true messiah and whose destinies even today are governed by Pharisees and scribes."

This, the authentic intellectual property of Nilus, differs markedly from all previous authorities. But where did our Nilus gain his wisdom? Let us hear what he says about this:

Through the Spirit of our Mother Church came my rebirth to a new life; from its Spirit came divine revelation concerning heavenly and earthly things. Mystery upon mystery revealed itself to my human weakness, mysteries in which the great power of God was made manifest. Only through this power did I comprehend that the essence of the world and all that it comprises is only to be fathomed in the light of divine Truth: there is and can be no absolute truth on earth; for the reign of truth, through the Second Coming of Christ, under a new heaven and upon a new earth, the Antichrist must first appear who shall be recognized by the Jews as the messiah, and by the world as tsar and master of all.

We see, from his unambiguous assurances, that Nilus owes his revelation to the highest possible source of truth, namely the Holy Spirit. He is in direct communication with the same.

Still, Nilus was plagued by weighty conundrums. How was it possible that the Antichrist should issue from the Jewish nation when he had to conquer the entire world and subject it to himself as tsar and master? The Jews were scattered, to all appearances a persecuted tribe, in a world still obviously composed of mighty states and nations. How could the insignificant descendant of the international ghetto find it possible to battle against such political powers? Such weighty doubts robbed Nilus of his sleep. The Holy Spirit, with whom he is in constant communication, decided to grant him a sign to dispel all his doubts. Thus, as Nilus expresses it so elegantly: "The advent of the Antichrist, the Second Coming of the Lord, and the end of the world shall not and must not be effected until the Holy Spirit prepares mankind in appropriate ways."

And what did the Holy Spirit do to remove the tormenting doubts of its loyal servant? It placed a document into his hands that irrefutably and unambiguously shows that the true facts coincide exactly with Nilus's doctrine.

In the preface to the second edition (1905) of the book published by the government printing office at Tsarskoe Selo near St. Petersburg, Nilus writes: "In the year 1901 there came into my possession through the agency of a friend a handwritten manuscript. In it is an unusually detailed and truthful account of the development of a world-spanning Masonic-Jewish conspiracy that shall lead our ruined world to its inevitable destruction. This manuscript, entitled the *Protocols of the Elders of Zion,* I transmit to all those who will to hear, to see, and to comprehend."

From the *Protocols* it is learned that the Jews, scattered all over the world and designating themselves as a persecuted tribe, in reality bestride the globe and command extraordinary powers. They rule not only in individual states but comprise a secret superworld government that compels all the heads of state, military, and civil administrations to obedience. Together with the world association of Freemasons, their slaves unto death, the Jews conspire by means of liberal institutions gradually to destroy all nations and to erect upon their ruins the Jewish world state, with a Jewish world leader at its pinnacle.

Is this not a total confirmation of Nilus's doctrine? Is not this Jewish world ruler none other than the expected Antichrist? And as the demands of the "Jews and Freemasons" — so all liberals in Russia are branded — became more insistent, was it not clear that the Antichrist stood before the gates and that the end of the world was nigh? Sergei Nilus therefore committed a highly patriotic act, in fact, earned the whole world's undying gratitude, when he raised his voice in warning and transmitted the *Protocols* to all those "who will to hear, to see, and to comprehend." He might have been permitted to hope that, in the nick of time, he had succeeded in opening the eyes of an insensible world, that it might yet avert a terrible end — the devil's rule on earth.

The Jews were actually pursuing such plans, of that there could be no doubt. For the *Protocols,* wrested away from them, was indeed a freely made confession of the Jews. Now, for the first time in history, the millennial secret of the Jewish people's plan to conquer the world saw the light of day. Let the whole human race take warning.

§

Let us now return to Nilus's thinking concerning the meaning of history.

KING SOLOMON,
FOUNDER OF THE SOCIETY OF THE ELDERS OF ZION

According to secret Jewish documents, it was in 929 B.C. that wise King Solomon, dwelling in the citadel of Zion in Jerusalem, worked out the Jewish people's plan for a bloodless conquest of the world in collaboration with other Jewish elders, or so Nilus assures us. "To the extent that historical events necessitated, his successors, whom he had initiated into the matter, revised and then completed the plan."

Now it is clear what the name "Elders of Zion" signifies. It was a secret league founded by King Solomon and other Jewish sages atop the citadel of Mount Zion 2,855 years ago in order, without shedding blood, to conquer the world for the Jewish people. This League of the Elders of Zion has absolutely nothing to do with the Zionists who met in Basel in 1897 to deliberate on the founding of a Jewish state in Palestine as a refuge for all Jews.

THE SERPENT SYMBOL

The question arises, however: how is the tiny Jewish people supposed to gather enough power to subject the entire world to itself and then to rule over it without bloodshed? Nilus has the answer. The Jews contrive the conquest of the world by means of the "cunning symbolic serpent." The serpent's tail rests on Zion, but the body, with head in front, slithers over the entire world. Coiling into the bosom of the states that it encounters, the serpent gnaws at and devours all non-Jewish state forces by means of liberal constitutions and economic dislocations. The serpent has already passed through seven stages of world history. Beginning with Greece in the Age of Pericles, it gnawed at the power and greatness of this land. The seventh stage was reached in St. Petersburg in 1881 (the year in which Tsar Alexander II was assassinated). With the return of the serpent's head to Zion, the symbolic snake will end its circuit through world history. Then it will have embraced all of Europe in its coils and, through Europe, all the world.

But this return of the serpent's head to Zion can only take place if all the powers of Europe are brought low by the destruction and devastation the Jewish people have everywhere brought with them, the moral degradation and ruin that always accompany liberalism.

It must be admitted that this whole train of thought is surrounded by such a depth and breadth of mysticism that we strive in vain to understand it. What are we to think of the symbolic serpent? Nilus presumably means the serpent in the Garden of Eden. Is it an earthly or a heavenly snake? Where does it dwell? What mortal has ever been deemed worthy to see it? How does the symbolic serpent spread liberalism in the state? And most important: where are these secret Jewish documents from which Nilus draws his science? What language are they in? When did they originate? Why has Nilus not published them, in the original language or in translation, so that the entire world could apprehend the truth of this precious evidence?

We have no answers for any of these questions. Apparently, we are left with no other alternative than to accept gullibly and naively all that Nilus tells us, ignoring our own human reason.

One category of Russians took careful note of the holy Nilus's revelations. These were the operatives of the Okhrana—the spies, go-betweens, eavesdroppers, back-stabbers, informers, and the whole race of vile, venal creatures among whom Nilus worked as a lowly official in the department overseeing foreign religious denominations. For this audience the doctrine of Nilus was an irreproachable revelation. The more such doctrines were spread, the more these people would have to do, and the more their significance and power in the world would mount.

To us ordinary mortals, however, the historical and philosophical views presented here leave no doubt as to the spiritual parentage of this Nilus. The cynical forger and liar brims with pious phrases and constantly drops the name of the Holy Spirit, indeed, is even shameless enough to claim direct contact with, and revelations from, the same. This flimflam must fill honest men with disgust, whether they are believers or unbelievers.

And German men have chosen this Nilus as their flag bearer. His clumsy forgery, vouched for only by his "good name," they have loosed upon the German people as a revelation of the deepest political secrets. Just as incredible is the fact that hundreds of thousands of German men and women believe this stuff, seek to have others believe it, and make it the basis for their political decisions.

But certainly the sterling Russian's German apostles, especially zur Beek, have not given their esteemed readers even a hint about the book *The Great in the Small*. That would be a bit too risky. Even the most gullible readers might balk at the famous story of the symbolic serpent slithering through world history, or the one about the League of the Elders of Zion founded by King Solomon 2,855 years ago and still dangerous to the entire non-Jewish world. Remaining silent about all this "wisdom" and putting only the *Protocols* before the respected public was certainly pragmatic. Notwithstanding this, the [*Protocols*] appeared as an addendum in the original Russian book, without which the forgery remains wholly senseless and incomprehensible.

We have seen that the translation by Gottfried zur Beek contains a series of falsifications that the translator of the Russian text of the *Protocols* — itself one long falsification — perpetrated on his own authority. It is difficult at this point to decide which is the greater misdeed: the suppression of *The Great in the Small* or the forgeries themselves. In either case, Gottfried zur Beek is "an honorable man." And he and the forger Sergei Nilus deserve one another.

TRUTHFULNESS AS THE PRIME GERMAN VIRTUE
Heinrich von Treitschke once identified truthfulness as "the best German virtue."[37] But here we are dealing with Germans who will-

fully embroil their own people in senseless lies. Building upon the crude forgery of a Russian police spy, they add their own new forgeries and bring them before a wide public. What ought we to think about parties that do not hesitate to use these sorts of weapons in politics? They can square it with their consciences that the public opinion of their people will be poisoned, poisoned perhaps for decades, by this witches' brew of lies, fraud, and superstition.

It would be a mistake to take comfort in the adage "Lies have short legs." Belief in a Jewish conspiracy to conquer the world and in the *Protocols* will not soon pass away. History teaches us that superstitious ideas of this sort live on for centuries, transmitted from generation to generation. This is especially so when an influential and self-serving stratum of society seeks to implant these beliefs in the unconscious of a people by means of vigorous, lasting agitation. It will require hard and persistent struggle to get free of them.

A HISTORICAL EXAMPLE

The following example, which echoes the current belief in the *Protocols,* illustrates the dangers of superstition.

The Fourth Lateran Council in 1215 established the dogma that bread and wine, consecrated by the priest and received by the faithful during Holy Communion, were transformed into the body and blood of Christ. Soon thereafter, crude physical superstitions sprang up among the people concerning the holy wafer. The people became convinced that the sacred host contained the body of Christ in the most literal sense. A few decades later, there arose the universal superstition that the Jews, who had crucified Christ and harbored an eternal hatred against Him, tempted Christians to steal the wafers and to sell them to Jews. The Jews then tormented the host with all the instruments of torture and drained off its blood so as to satisfy their insatiable thirst for revenge against Christ. Year in and year out for five centuries, a few hundred Jews in the Catholic countries were sent to the scaffold, burned alive, or drowned because of their desecration of the host. At the site of the crime, the tortured host always worked miracles and soon a church or cloister was built, usually christened "Sacred Blood," which drew the sumptuous gifts of pilgrims from all over the world.

As late as 19 July 1510, seven years before the appearance of Martin Luther, there occurred near the present site of the Frankfurter Allee in Berlin the public burning of thirty-nine Jews. After a trial lasting several months, the accused confessed, under torture, to having beaten for hours with a hammer upon a consecrated wafer the size of a penny and as thin as paper; then they punctured it with a butcher knife until streams of blood poured forth.

This was probably the last trial for host desecration in Germany, for the spreading Protestant Reformation soon put an end to this whole conceptual world. But in Catholic countries such as Poland, such trials were almost annual occurrences for centuries. Thus, in 1556 six Jews were burned for this crime in the little town of Sochaczew. In 1637 the people of Kraków cast forty Jews into the Vistula, of whom seven drowned. In Poznan in 1399, thirteen Jews were burned alive for host desecration, and the Jewish community was forced to pay an annual fine for an unlimited period. At the beginning of the seventeenth century, the Carmelites of Poznan discovered the table upon which the Jews had committed their sacrilege in 1399. And — what a miracle! — there were still traces of the copious blood siphoned from the wafer by the Jews. At the end of the eighteenth century, shortly before the First Partition of Poland [1772], the Jews of Poznan were still paying to the city treasury the fine leveled upon them in 1399. So astonishingly stubborn is a superstition.

Yet how easily a little reflection would have sufficed to reveal the ridiculousness of this accusation. Had the Jews ever been able to draw blood from a consecrated wafer, such a miracle would have convinced them of the truth of Christianity. Surely, they would have accepted baptism en masse rather than continuing to defile sacred hosts and being burned alive.

It must be acknowledged that this superstition was supported by the frequent appearance of "bleeding hosts." From time to time, these fine, penny-sized wafers of unleavened wheat flour exhibited large, deep-red, pearl-shaped drops. Thus, anyone might be convinced by the evidence of his own eyes. What could the drops be but the blood from the body of the Lord? And the infamous Jews, those eternal enemies of Christ, why should they not covet this blood?

The belief in the Jews' desecration of the host might still bedevil the intellectual nether regions, like the superstition that Jews require the blood of slaughtered Christian children for their matzo, were it not for a scientific discovery, made in the middle of the nineteenth century, that the drops of "blood" on the host had a natural explanation. On 26 October 1848 the natural scientist [Christian Gottfried] Ehrenberg gave a lecture at the Berlin Academy of Sciences in which he showed that a type of bacteria was responsible for the appearance of "blood" on the host and other similar objects; this microbe had been discovered as early as 1819 by the Italian [Ernesto] Setti, but it had not been fully investigated by Ehrenberg until 1848. "Hence, it follows that on the basis of this phenomenon the Jews were unjustly accused of host desecration. I could easily reproduce this phenomenon on wafers. It also thrives well on cooked rice kept in warm, covered dishes." From this moment, science put an end to a centuries-old superstition that had claimed countless human sacrifices.

THE CASE OF LÉO TAXIL

Here is an example from more recent times that shows how relentless, shameless agitation can humbug even responsible, high-ranking men on the basis of the most ridiculous fairy tales. Older readers will recall the tremendous world sensation created in Paris in 1897 when Léo Taxil unmasked his own swindles. For more than twelve years, the world had gasped at Taxil's revelations about the machinations of the Freemasons, their black masses, their customs, which held all religion and morality in contempt, their criminal deeds and plans. Taxil published countless pieces in many languages on this inexhaustibly gruesome subject, and they brought him enormous wealth. He even succeeded in misleading the pope and the highest dignitaries of the church, men noted throughout the world for their political intelligence and having the best sources of information at their disposal. Finally, on 19 April 1897, the cynical adventurer and swindler Léo Taxil admitted to the whole world that it had all been a monstrous fraud. . . .

Were it not for well-documented facts, [the whole episode]

would seem scarcely credible in the modern world. [It] is probable that the *Protocols* was first sketched out in the circles around Taxil.[38]

§

If we do not move quickly to choke off the roots of the superstitious belief in the *Protocols,* who can assure us that it will not continue to befog the understanding of simple men, poison their hearts, and pervert their common sense for decades, perhaps for centuries to come?

1. Claiming an ancient lineage, Freemasonry took organized form in England in 1717 and spread to the Continent after 1730. The original intent of English Masons seems to have been universalist, the acceptance of all who acknowledged God and the moral law, no matter the particular religion. Elsewhere, the emphasis on Christianity as a qualification for membership and the expensive entrance fees weakened the universalist creed. In 1738 Pope Clement XII excommunicated the Masons as the carriers of heresy and enemies of the Catholic Church. The Abbé Augustin Barruel, alluded to by Segel, traced the French Revolution back to a plot hatched by the Knights Templar, who, surviving their attempted extermination in 1314, reconstituted themselves as a secret society of Freemasons to wreak vengeance on all monarchs and the papacy. They supposedly sought to establish a world republic by means of preaching liberty to the masses. In fact, many Freemasons died at the hands of republicans during the Red Terror. Nor were antimonarchical principles automatic among them.

In another French innovation, the Masonic conspiracy became a Judeo-Masonic conspiracy in the 1820s. That Jews at no time played a disproportionately large role in Freemasonry and that lodges outside England and Holland either refused to accept them as members, or did so grudgingly, were facts that did not disturb the creators of this myth. In 1922, the Communist International (Comintern) ruled out simultaneous membership in the Masons and the party, objecting especially to the heavily bourgeois membership of the lodges. But the obscure origins of Freemasonry, along with its mystical rituals, international organization, and Enlightenment principles, rendered it continuously suspicious to the right. Conservative nationalists, racists, and churchmen saw Freemasonry as the "handmaiden of Bolshevism." It was banned in the interwar years in Hungary, Italy, Spain, Germany, Portugal, and Turkey. During World War II a special anti-Masonic section of the German SS ferreted out and closed down numerous lodges.

The Illuminati, an obscure group of anticlerical Bavarians brought together in 1776 by Adam Weishaupt (1748–1830) "to emancipate all mankind from religious and political slavery," has proved equally fascinating to conspiracy theorists. Although the society has been blamed for every revolution from 1789 to the present day, whatever real influence the Illuminati enjoyed ended in the 1780s.

On the linkup of Jews and Masons, see Katz, *Jews and Freemasons in Europe*; on conspiracy thinking in history, see Roberts, *Mythology of the Secret Societies*; Rogalla von Bieberstein, *Die These von der Verschwörung*.

2. Gougenot des Mousseaux was neither the first nor the last Frenchman to describe a Jewish world conspiracy. He was preceded by the socialist disciple of Charles Fourier, Alphonse Toussenel (1813–85), who condemned the "financial feudalism" of Jewish bankers. (*Les Juifs rois de l'époque*; Paris, 1845). Gougenot's most important successor was Edouard-Adolphe Drumont (1844–1917) whose book *La France juive* (1886) and newspaper *La Libre Parole* reached a very large audience with tales of far-flung historical and contemporary Jewish conspiracies. France was therefore well prepared to provide the milieu for the production of the *Protocols*.

3. The Antichrist, according to Christian legend, was the spawn of a Jewish prostitute impregnated by Satan who was born in Babylon. The enemy of Christ and of all Christians and the embodiment of absolute evil, the countermessiah would be crowned in Jerusalem and restore the Jewish Temple; he would attract numerous followers but was to be defeated in a terrible battle as a prelude to the Second Coming of Christ.

4. Friedrich Wichtl, *Weltfreimauerei, Weltrevolution, Weltrepublik: Eine Untersuchung über Ursprung und Endziele des Weltkrieges* (Munich, 1919). "A book that explains all and tells us against whom we must fight," the nineteen-year-old Heinrich Himmler noted in his diary (quoted in Rogalia von Bieberstein, *Die These von Verschwürung*, p.211). Wichtl's book was reprinted as recently as 1983.

5. The assassination of the reformist Tsar Alexander II on 13 March 1881

by a member of the terrorist group the People's Will led to a wave of anti-Jewish riots. Gavrilo Princip, a Serbian nationalist, murdered the heir-apparent of the Austro-Hungarian Empire, Archduke Franz Ferdinand (1863–1914), along with his wife in Sarajevo on 28 June 1914. The assassination set off the "July Crisis," which led to the outbreak of World War I.

6. The declaration issued under the name of Arthur Balfour, foreign secretary in Lloyd George's wartime government, on 2 November 1917, promised British support for the establishment of a *Jewish national home*, not a Jewish state, in Palestine. The Balfour Declaration, which was generally perceived as the result of powerful Jewish influence, contained the important proviso that the civil and religious rights of the existing non-Jewish communities would be safeguarded. In view of Arab unrest when the British mandate for Palestine went into effect in 1923, the declaration was interpreted in ways that hindered Jewish settlement. British policy culminated in the White Paper of May 1939, which severely restricted Jewish immigration to seventy-five thousand over a five-year period. It thus essentially sealed off a possible site of refuge for massive numbers of Jews fleeing Nazi persecution.

7. In Hebrew the word *goyim* designates all the nations of the world other than Israel. For Jews, this originally neutral term for Gentiles acquired disparaging connotations. *Goy* (singular) became synonymous with anti-semite.

8. Under the motto Autocracy, Orthodoxy, Nationality, Tsar Nicholas I (1825–55) ruled the Russian Empire with an iron hand, crushing liberalism, controlling the universities, intensifying censorship, and strengthening the secret police. Tsar Ivan IV (1530–84) earned the epithet "the Terrible" largely because of the unrelenting cruelty with which he enforced his rule over the Russian nobles, the boyars.

9. The secrecy attributed to the Zionist Congress at Basel in the *Protocols* is vital to the myth. However, Herzl's opening speech to the congress could not have been more emphatic on the need for openness: "We Zionists do not want a solution to the Jewish question through some international agency but through international discussion. With us it cannot be a matter for secret societies, interventions, or machinations but only candid discussions under the constant control of public opinion." Quoted in Bein, *Die Judenfrage*, 1:329–30, note.

10. Ludwig Müller von Hausen (1851–1929) was by this time a retired army captain and editor of the antisemitic monthly *Auf Vorposten* (On outpost duty). Before the war he was one of the chief organizers of the Alliance against the Arrogance of Jewry, a body that came to be closely associated with the Pan-German League. For an English translation of excerpts from several sections of the *Protocols* and one of the Alliance's earlier "educational" proclamations, see Levy, ed., *Antisemitism in the Modern World*, pp.124, 129–30, 149–65.

11. Prince Otto zu Salm (1867–1941) was indeed a high-ranking aristocrat and right-wing politician, former president of the German Naval League and leading member of the Pan-German League. Even before the war ended or the *Protocols* had arrived in Germany, a Salm speech in the Prussian upper house on 9 July 1918 drew attention to the "Jewish-Freemason international," blaming it for the war and for every revolution of modern times and identifying Lenin and Trotsky not only as Jews but as Freemasons too.

In the last days of World War I, Kaiser Wilhelm II, having become the symbol at home and abroad for the continuing war, fled over the border to the Netherlands. He remained an exile in Doorn until his death in 1941. Joachim Albrecht was the youngest of Wilhelm's six sons.

12. *Pogrom,* in Russian, means devastation. Until recently, the term described exclusively the organized or spontaneous massacres of Jews. In Russia the worst pogroms occurred in 1881, 1903, 1905, and during the civil war in areas controlled by the anti-Bolshevik White Russian armies, especially the Ukraine.

13. One of the most prolific antisemitic publishers of the imperial and Weimar eras, Theodor Fritsch (1852–1933) is best known as editor of the *Handbuch der Judenfrage* (Handbook of the Jewish question), 48th ed. (Leipzig, 1943), and an antisemitic journal with intellectual pretensions, *Hammer: Blätter für deutschen Sinn* (The hammer: pages for German sensibilities; Leipzig, 1902–40). The "old master," as he was called, lived long enough to see the Nazis achieve power and to be eulogized by the Nazi elite. Typically, Fritsch sent out half an edition of one of his works free of charge to youth groups, influential individuals, Sunday schools, and various nationalist organizations; the interest thus drummed up usually sufficed to sell the other half and then finance a new edition.

14. A career soldier, Erich Ludendorff (1865–1937) became a national hero during World War I as the chief of staff and brains behind Field Marshal Paul von Hindenburg. A relentless enemy of democracy, he participated in two right-wing coup attempts against the Weimar Republic and served as a racist–nationalist Reichstag deputy (1924–28). In a series of publications in the late 1920s, however, he and his wife, Mathilde, fell into an elaborate form of Teuton worship, identifying Jews, Jesuits, and Freemasons as the common enemies of the supposed Aryan race. By the time of his death, Ludendorff had exhausted his influence, even for the radical right.

15. Segel is slightly off on the complicated history of the book's publication. Maurice Joly's *Dialogue aux enfers entre Machiavel et Montesquieu, ou la politique de Machiavel au XIXe siècle: Par un Contemporain* first appeared anonymously in 1864 with a Geneva imprimatur, but it had in fact been printed in Brussels. Smuggled into France, where it was illegal to criticize the regime, the book led to Joly's arrest and jailing.

16. Ferdinand Lassalle (1825–64), the son of a Jewish merchant, along with Karl Marx (1818–83), was instrumental in establishing the revolutionary German labor movement. Lassalle's contribution was skillful agitation and the organization of the first significant German trade union. According to Lassalle's conception, after workers wrested the vote from the ruling class, socialism was to be achieved gradually by means of legislation that would turn the state into an ally of the German worker. A brilliant journalist and orator, he died in a duel just as the movement was beginning to make great strides.

17. Leon Trotsky (1879–1940), born Lev Davidovich Bronstein, was the most prominent Bolshevik of Jewish background. In the struggle to succeed Lenin, he lost out to Joseph Stalin and was exiled and eventually murdered on Stalin's orders.

18. On Napoleon III and the Commune of Paris, see note 25.

19. Count Ernst zu Reventlow (1869–1943), a declassé nobleman, was active in right-wing politics and journalism before 1914, an advocate of imperialist foreign policy, antisemitism, and authoritarian rule. He was a close associate of Gottfried zur Beek and the Alliance against the Arrogance of Jewry, the organization that first published the *Protocols* in Germany. Initially critical of Adolf Hitler, Reventlow joined the Nazis in 1924 and was one of the few important prewar antisemites to play a significant role in the party.

Theodor Herzl (1860–1904) was born in Budapest and worked as a journalist in Vienna. His experience of the Dreyfus affair and the intense antisemitism it provoked in the mid-1890s convinced him that Jewish assimilation would not solve "the Jewish problem." As an alternative, he began speaking, writing, and negotiating for the establishment of a Jewish state. While the highly assimilated Herzl's view of the future Jewish state was largely political, his great rival, the Russian Jew Asher Ginsburg (1856–1927), known as Ahad Ha'am ("one of the people"), saw it as the cultural and spiritual center of a revived Jewish nation.

20. The charge of ritual murder, or "the blood libel," which emerged in the middle of the twelfth century, asserted that Jews required the blood of Christians, usually children, for ritual or bizarre magical purposes. The many variants of the charge usually included sadistic cruelty practiced upon a helpless child, "factual" details provided by a Jewish witness to enhance credibility, placement of the deed at Easter and Passover, and reference to the killing of Christ, which the murder was intended to celebrate anew.

The ritual murder allegation often led to violence against Jews and occasionally provoked more widespread disorders. In the thirteenth century, when the charge was particularly rife, Holy Roman Emperor Frederick II instructed a commission of high churchmen to settle the question as to whether or not the Jews required Christian blood. His Golden Bull of 1236 declared the charges groundless. A decade later, Pope Innocent IV also issued an official pronouncement that acquitted the Jews of "blood guilt" and condemned the motives of those who raised the charge.

But the myth had taken hold of popular imagination and has never wholly disappeared. At the end of the nineteenth century, several ritual murder trials, invested now with overtones of sexual depravity, seized public attention. From 1891 to 1900, no fewer than 120 stories of ritual murder received extensive coverage in German antisemitic newspapers. The "blood libel" surfaced in upstate New York in the 1920s and in Argentina as recently as the early 1960s.

21. Segel was apparently unaware of the very first publication of the forgery, in abbreviated form, in Pavolachi Krushevan's Russian-language newspaper, *Znamia* (The banner), between 26 August and 7 September 1903. Segel lists the following as the documentary basis for his study: photocopies of the *Protocols* as an addendum to Nilus's *The Great in the Small*

(1905), housed in the British Museum of London; the 1911 edition of Nilus's book, on which zur Beek supposedly based his (German) translation, made newly available in the anti-Bolshevik Russian journal *Luch Sveta* (Beam of light; Berlin, 1920); a French translation of 1921 by Roger Lambelin also made from the 1911 edition of Nilus; an American translation from the 1917 edition of Nilus, published in Boston (1920). These are the four editions from the Russian originals, along with their various commentaries, to which Segel refers. Additional material, much of it in facsimile, came from Polish, British, French, American, and Russian variants.

22. The oily and sinister Pyotr Ivanovich Rachkovsky, chief of the foreign branch of the Okhrana, who died in 1911 ("killed on the orders of the Elders of Zion," according to zur Beek) is suspected by the modern authority on the *Protocols* of having been the most likely instigator of its fabrication. His numerous attempts to discredit liberal hoax organizations, or radical movements by associating them with Jews often involved planting phony letters or articles in the European press, and other dirty tricks. For his career, see Cohn, *Warrant for Genocide*, pp.78–83.

23. Herman Bernstein was an American diplomat whose *History of a Lie* (1921) was one of the earliest exposés of the *Protocols*.

24. At the time of the revolution, the total Jewish population of France was less than fifty thousand. Of these, eight thousand were Sephardim, descendants of Portuguese and Spanish Jews who had fled the Inquisition, living in the southern cities of Bordeaux, Bayonne, and Marseilles; a few thousand Sephardic Jews had also made their way to Paris by this time. The rest, Ashkenazim, far less assimilated in terms of French culture, lived in Alsace and Lorraine.

25. Louis Napoleon Bonaparte (1808–73) was the nephew of the great Napoleon. After a checkered career abroad, he returned to France during the Revolution of 1848, and through adroit exploitation of his illustrious name he was elected president of the Second French Republic. Although constitutionally limited to one term, he staged a coup on 2 December 1851 that led ultimately to the creation of the Second French Empire and his new title, Napoleon III, emperor of the French. The European left regarded the coup as a definitive end to the revolutionary movement of 1848, identifying Napoleon as the destroyer of democratic emancipation. The legitimist right, as Segel points out, despised him as a usurper. His style of rule relied

on the control of public opinion, an adventurist foreign policy, censorship, and secret surveillance of political enemies. Bonapartism used many of the trappings of democracy, such as universal suffrage and the plebiscite, but was essentially manipulative and anything but democratic. Measured by the standards of a Hitler or a Stalin, Napoleon III's reign seems fairly tame, free as it was from mass murder and the concentration camp. However, many modern historians regard his rule as precedent-setting for the totalitarian regimes of the twentieth century.

The Second Empire came to an end in France's humiliating military defeat during the Franco-Prussian War of 1870–71. Shortly after Napoleon's capture during the war, a revolution broke out in Paris. For ten weeks before its bloody suppression, the Commune of Paris presented the spectacle of a European city democratically ruled by representatives of the lower classes. In the street fighting that ended the commune, atrocities and the wanton destruction of property poisoned relations between the classes. Long afterward, the episode of the commune continued to summon up nightmarish memories for the possessing classes all over Europe.

26. From the reign of Alexander I (1801–25) until the Revolution of 1917, the Pale of Permanent Jewish Settlement defined the areas of the Russian Empire in which Jews were legally allowed to live. The lands annexed during the partitions of Poland (1772, 1793, 1795) and fifteen provinces stretching from Lithuania to the southern Ukraine constituted one huge ghetto designed to keep Jews out of the Russian heartland.

27. The Russo-Japanese War broke out in 1904 over imperialist conflicts in Manchuria and Korea. Japanese attempts to negotiate the problem were rebuffed by the war party in St. Petersburg, which hoped to use the confidently expected victory to extinguish revolutionary ferment in Russia. But Japan soundly defeated the Russian army at Port Arthur and Mukden and sank the Russian fleet in the Straits of Tsushima. The Japanese victory shocked the world and led directly to the Russian Revolution of 1905.

28. Although Segel is correct to point out that zur Beek "edited" the League of Nations into his version of the *Protocols,* the idea of a society of nations to prevent war was centuries-old before President Woodrow Wilson incorporated it in the last of his Fourteen Points in January 1918. The covenant of the league established a governing structure much like that of its successor, the United Nations; a world court to arbitrate national conflicts;

and many other institutions that undertook humanitarian enterprises. When the United States refused to ratify the Versailles settlement ending World War I, it also rejected membership in the league, a very serious blow to its effectiveness. Membership, at first confined to the victors in the war, was extended to the USSR in 1934 and Germany in 1926. German rightists relentlessly resisted the league, and Hitler withdrew Germany from membership in 1933. The League of Nations proved unable to prevent Japanese, Italian, and German aggression.

29. In 1878 a French company under the leadership of Ferdinand de Lesseps, builder of the Suez Canal, acquired a concession for a canal across the Isthmus of Panama. The project seized the imagination of many French investors but soon ran into problems that required enormous new sums. As public investment slackened, de Lesseps hired a Jewish fund-raiser. When the French government refused his petition for a national lottery, the fund-raiser employed new tactics, including hefty bribes for government officials and legislators, doled out by a Jewish public relations man. When the lottery was finally wangled but yielded less than expected, de Lesseps resigned and his company went bankrupt. A half million investors lost their money, totaling fifteen hundred million francs, of which half had gone for bribes. All this came to light when the main culprits implicated each other in the press. In the uproar that followed, one of them committed suicide, the other fled France; five former cabinet ministers, along with twelve parliamentarians, a chief of police, and several bankers were investigated by the police. The republic's prestige suffered serious damage.

30. Contrary to what Segel says in the next paragraph, this bit of fantasy has been used to help establish the time and place (Paris circa 1898) for the creation (though not the publication) of the *Protocols*. Although subway construction was still an exotic idea for many Europeans, the Paris Métro concession had been granted in 1894; the first line opened in 1900. The leading French antisemite, Edouard Drumont (1844–1917), claimed, without proof, that most of the shareholders in the Métro were Jewish.

31. Field Marshal Horatio Herbert Kitchener (1850–1916) was aboard the H.M.S. *Hampshire,* on his way to confer with Russian leaders, when the ship struck a German mine near the Orkney Islands; he and many of his staff drowned. The "stab-in-the-back" myth (*Dolchstoss*) asserted that the German army had not been defeated in the field in World War I. Rather, it had

been betrayed at home by socialist and democratic revolutionaries, Jews, or the dupes of Jews. The myth served to exonerate Germany's ruling elite during the war of any responsibility for the military catastrophe. The radical right employed it to condemn all those in the Weimar Republic who accepted the consequences of defeat.

32. Otto Friedrich, *Die Protokolle der Weisen von Zion: das Buch der Fälschungen* (The Protocols of the Elders of Zion: the book of forgeries; Lübeck, 1920).

33. For three days in April 1903, Kishinev, a district capital, was the scene of murder, rape, and torture. According to an official report, more than fifty Jews were killed and more than five hundred injured; hundreds of homes and shops were plundered and vandalized. It was widely believed at the time that the tsar's government had prepared the pogrom by sponsoring antisemitic propaganda and agitation and that its agents actually led the mob. More certain is that local authorities — Kishinev was administered by a governor with troops at his disposal — supported antisemitic organizations and deliberately maximized the carnage by postponing the use of force to reestablish order. See the testimony of S. D. Urusov, who replaced the Russian governor at Kishinev and who held the central administration morally, if not materially, responsible for the violence, in James Cracraft, ed., *Major Problems in the History of Imperial Russia* (Lexington MA, 1993).

34. Sir John Retcliffe [Hermann Goedsche], *Das Geheimnis der jüdischen Weltherrschaft: Aus einem Werke des vorigen Jahrhunderts, das von den Juden aufgekauft wurde und aus dem Buchhandel verschwand* (Berlin, 1919).

35. In his longer study of 1924, Segel includes thirty-two pages of side-by-side comparisons. He also acknowledges that Philip Graves, the *Times* of London correspondent in Constantinople, was the first to have detected some of the plagiarized examples cited. Norman Cohn calculates that zur Beek lifted more than 160 passages, or two-fifths of the *Protocols,* from Joly's book. With less than a dozen exceptions, the order of the stolen passages also follows Joly slavishly. "It is in fact as clear a case of plagiarism — and of faking — as one could well desire." See Cohn, *Warrant for Genocide,* pp. 74–75.

36. Grigori Yefimovich Rasputin (1872–1916) owed his position to being able to stop the bleeding of the hemophiliac tsarevich who was the son of Nicholas and Alexandra. The negative influence on personnel and

policy he was deemed to be exercising through the tsaritsa led a group of high-ranking noblemen to poison, shoot, and then dump him in the Neva River in December 1916.

37. Segel invokes the name of the doyen of nationalist historians, Heinrich von Treitschke (1834–96), to make a general point about the responsibility of respected intellectuals for the spread of antisemitic ideology. Treitschke, in all likelihood, would have scorned the fantasies of the *Protocols,* yet he had written that "the Jews are our misfortune" in his influential booklet *Ein Wort über unser Judenthum* (A word about our Jews; 1880). His lectures at the University of Berlin and his widely read political commentary stressed the danger posed by Jews to the German nation. His enormous prestige influenced a generation of university students and ideologues and helped legitimize political antisemitism in Germany.

38. Taxil enjoyed the confidence of several high-ranking churchmen, but his main and most gullible audience was the poorly educated rural clergy of France and Italy. To them, he revealed that the head of the U.S. Freemasons had installed a telephone system with devils as operators in order to maintain constant communication with seven world capitals. Taxil confined his fantasies to the Freemasons, but others in his circle made the connection to the Jews, and it was there, in all likelihood, that the most important initial sketch of the *Protocols* came into being. See Cohn, *Warrant for Genocide,* p.48.

APPENDIX

THE FIRST PROTOCOL

I have framed the basic principles of our league, in general and in particular, without regard to scientific considerations. I describe our doctrines and our system as it appears to us and to non-Jews.

I assert that men with evil motives outnumber those with good character. In the administration of the state, therefore, more can be achieved by force and unscrupulousness than by scientific discussions. Every man strives for power; every individual wants to be master of his own decisions and deeds; each would be master of himself (a dictator), if only he could. This striving after power is so strong that there is scarcely a man who would not be ready to sacrifice the common good for his own personal advantage.

What instincts rule over the beasts of prey that feed upon the blood of men? What have been their actions and desires through all time? Since the rise of human society, beasts of prey in human form have seized raw, blind force for themselves. From this I conclude that *force* alone is the determining factor, no matter that it be veiled and disguised. Thus it follows that the basic law of existence rests wholly on the idea: Right is based on force, on strength.

The Idea of Freedom — Freethinking
Civil freedom is an idea, a concept, but not a fact. This idea transforms itself as soon as the power of a nation is suppressed and

From Gottfried zur Beek [Ludwig Müller], *Die Geheimnisse der Weisen von Zion,* 4th ed. (Charlottenburg, 1920), pp.68–81, 91–92, 94, 101–5, 109–10, 112–13.

strangled, as soon as a party striving after dominance seeks to force its will upon the countermovement. This task becomes essentially easier when the opponent is himself contaminated with a false concept of "freedom" and yields his power on account of this incorrect notion. On this is based the victory of our doctrine: when the reins slide along the ground and leadership is lacking, the accomplished licentiousness ends quickly, for a new hand draws in the reins. A new domination steps into the place of the old, which was robbed of its power by freethinking.

Gold, Faith in God, Self-government

In our day, when the genuine freethinkers govern the state, the power of gold is the sole determining factor. There was a time when faith in God governed. The concept of freedom was still without system. No one understood how to exploit it for his purposes. No nation can exist for even the shortest time when it does not create a *rational* self-government, without which it sinks into licentiousness. From this moment there enters inner divisiveness, issuing in economic battles in the wake of which governments fall; gradually mob rule takes the rudder.

Domination of Money

A government finding itself under the influence of internal upheavals, or one that is at the mercy of external enemies because of the disordered conditions in its own land, must be undoubtedly consigned to oblivion. Then it is in our power. The dominance of money, over which we alone dispose, extends a straw to the government that it must grasp for good or ill if it wants to keep from sinking helplessly into the abyss.

To those freethinkers who believe such considerations to be immoral, I say: every realm has two enemies. If it is allowable to employ immoral methods in the struggle against the external enemy, for example, concealment of intentions or a sudden attack, attacking at night or with overwhelming superiority of forces, can one say it is morally impermissible to use such methods against the worst [internal] enemy, the destroyer of social harmony and economic well-being?

The Masses and Lawlessness

Can a man of sound and logical intelligence hope to rule the masses of a nation successfully if he merely employs rational principles and logical arguments when the possibility of contradiction exists in the people? Would an even half-way intelligent people be thereby easier to govern? If such a man relied exclusively on minor measures — on old customs, traditions, sentiments, and emotional dogmas, the masses would divide and reject such a government. For the masses have no sense for rational exhortation. Every action of the masses depends upon an accidental or artificially constructed majority. Ignorant of the artifices of statecraft, they are carried along into foolish decisions, and thus the seed of lawlessness is planted within the state.

Statecraft and the Moral Law

Statecraft and the moral law have not the slightest to do with one another. A ruler who wants to rule by the moral law understands nothing about statecraft and is never for a moment secure upon his throne. He who would rule must labor with slyness, cunning, evil, hypocrisy. High moral character — openness, honor, honesty — these are the reefs of statecraft upon which the best will founder because the enemy makes use of different and truly more effective measures. Let these character traits be the hallmarks and principles of non-Jewish realms. We can never under any condition labor with such wrong-headed principles.

Our right lies in strength. "Strength" is a limited expression, not a universally valid concept. The word in itself never signifies more than: "Give me what I want so that it may be clear and self-evident to all the world that I am stronger than you."

Where does right begin? Where does it end? In a state where power is badly managed and laws and governors are rendered impersonal by freethinking [civil] rights, I shall create a new right. [I shall] demolish all institutions according to the right of the stronger, lay hands upon the law, transform all governing bodies, and become master of them. The power of these rights shall voluntarily transfer to us — because of freethinking.

The Invulnerability of Jewish Freemasonry

While at present all the powers have begun to totter, ours will be more invulnerable than any of the others because it will be invisible. Thus it shall remain unshakable until that time when it has become so empowered that no act of violence can repress it.

Out of the transitory calamities that we must now cause, there will emerge the benefaction of an unshakable government that shall reestablish the regulated development of national existence, undisturbed by freethinking. The results justify the means. Thus we shall direct our plans less by attention to the good and moral than by the necessary and useful.

Before us lies a plan, the lines of which are drawn according to the rules of war. We cannot deviate from it without endangering the labor of many centuries.

The Masses Are Blind

To achieve the goal of common efforts, we must learn to grasp the worthlessness, inconstancy, and vacillation of the masses. We must realize their incapacity to understand the questions of state life and their own welfare. We must comprehend that the great masses of the people are blind and wholly without understanding and that they willy-nilly stagger from right to left, backward and forward. A blind man cannot lead the blind without leading them into the abyss. Consequently, even the "inquisitive" and creative among the masses can never perform as leaders in governing the states. Even when they supposedly possess some intelligence, they are still not fit to act as trailblazers and leaders of the masses. They will attain to no other goal than the ruin of the entire people.

Only a personality educated to self-mastery from youth can recognize and act upon the great tendencies and principles of statecraft.

Party Strife

A people that delivers itself to the upstarts from out of the masses destroys its own structure by party battles, by the struggle for the leading positions of power, by the hunting after honors and dignities, and by the disorders and movements arising from all this. Is it possible that the masses can judge without prejudice, peacefully and matter-of-factly, that they can guide the destiny of the land without regard to purely personal interests? Can they defend the realm against external foes? That is senseless, for to distribute governance of the state among so many personalities, so many heads from out of the masses, will sacrifice its unity and it will become nonviable and powerless.

Only under the leadership of a self-controlled personality can the state be directed in full clarity and good order; only thus can the whole body politic labor in peace. From this it follows that the most appropriate form of the state for a country is found when the direction lies in the hands of a single responsible personality. Without unqualified power, no state system can thrive upon a moral basis. This basis cannot rest upon the masses but rather on the competent leader, be he who he may. The masses consist of barbarians who bring their coarseness and barbarity to bear at every opportunity. As soon as the masses seize power for themselves, they fall into lawlessness, the highest degree of barbarity.

Alcohol, Humanism, Vice
Observe the drunkards, befogged by alcohol. They believe themselves to possess the right to unlimited pleasure, which they confuse with the concept of freedom. From that idea we take leave for all time. The non-Jewish peoples are befogged with alcohol; their youths are infatuated with humanism and premature vices. To these they have been led by our agents, administrators, teachers, servants, governesses to the rich, educational institutions, and so forth, as well as by our women in pleasure resorts and public houses. Among these I also count the so-called society ladies, who willfully ape the example of vice and ostentation.

Principles of the Jewish Freemason Lodges
Our slogan is *Power and Artifice!* Power alone wrests the victory in questions of state, that is, when it is in the possession of personalities who have something to say in the state. Force forms the basis, but cunning and fraud work as the means to power for such govern-

ments as are not willing to lay their crowns at the feet of the representatives of a new power. These are the only means to the goal that hovers before us. Therefore, we must not shrink from bribery, fraud, or treason if they serve for the attainment of our plans. In statecraft we must be clever enough not to shrink from uncanny methods, if power and subjection be achieved thereby.

Terror
Our realm, which is founded on the paths of peaceful conquest, will replace the terrors of war with less visible but all the more effective punishments. It must institute a reign of terror in order to compel blind, unconditional obedience. Stern, pitiless, and ruthless measures are the best props of state power. Not alone for advantage but above all in the name of duty and for the sake of victory, we must hold firmly to the employment of force and cunning. . . . It is not only in the scientific evaluation of means, but above all in their ruthless and merciless application that our predominance, our superiority, shall be secured. It shall suffice to know that we are merciless and that we understand how to compel obedience.

Liberty, Equality, Fraternity
Already in antiquity we allowed the call for Liberty, Equality, Fraternity to echo from the ranks of the peoples. Since that time, these words have been endlessly repeated in the most varied disturbances and upheavals. Sometimes the intentions have been honorable, to bring actual well-being and true freedom of the personality to the world; sometimes it has just been to satisfy the vanity of the masses. Not even the intelligent and clever non-Jews have recognized the inner contradictions in these words. They have not said that there can be no equality, no freedom in nature. All of nature rests upon the inequality of forces, characteristics, peculiarities. Nature is subject to eternal laws. It is clear that the masses are a blind force, and the chosen upstarts are as blind as the masses themselves. The initiated, even if he is a fool, can govern, while the uninitiated, even when he is high-minded, can understand nothing about statecraft. All these things are forgotten by the non-Jews.

Principle of Princely Government
[On the non-Jews] depended the principle of princely government. The father bequeathed his knowledge of statecraft to the son, so that it was known only to members of the dynasty and none could betray the secrets to the peoples ruled over. In time the sense of the true content of statecraft was lost in the transmission, and this contributed to the success of our cause.

Abolishing the Privileges of the Non-Jewish Nobility
In all the corners of the world, with the help of our secret societies, the slogan Liberty, Equality, Fraternity led gigantic crowds to our ranks and carried our banners to victory. Those words were the worms that gnawed at the welfare of non-Jews, everywhere undermining peace, calm, community, common values, and thereby destroying the foundation of their domination. Gentlemen, you see the consequences that have served the triumph of our cause. *They gave us the possibility of playing out the highest trump: the annihilation of noble privilege, or, better said, the actual system of non-Jewish noble dominance, which has been the only means of defense of the non-Jewish peoples and states against us.*

The New Nobility
On the ruins of the old blood and family nobility we have set the nobility of our educated and at its tip, the money nobility. The standard of this new nobility lies in wealth, which depends upon us, and in the teachings disseminated by our secret associations.

Calculating Human Weaknesses
Our triumph was made all the easier in that we could exploit people useful to us by working on the most impressionable side of human intelligence: with consideration to money, greed, and the insatiable desire for gain. If we seize upon the right moment, all the extraordinarily numerous human weaknesses are suited to paralyze the powers of decision making. Those who best understand how to exploit human weaknesses are thus enabled to enslave the wills of men.

The concept of freedom made it possible to convince the masses that the government was nothing more than the deputies for those who possessed the land, that is, the people. The people therefore felt competent to change [governments] as one would change gloves.

Changes in the parliament delivered it into our power. It is elected or not, at our discretion.

BIBLIOGRAPHY

WORKS ABOUT THE *PROTOCOLS OF THE ELDERS OF ZION*

Aronsfeld, C. C. "The *Protocols* among the Arabs." *Patterns of Prejudice* 9 (July/August 1975): 17–19.

Bach, H. I. "Projections of the '*Protocols*': The Guilt Feeling in Antisemitism." *Patterns of Prejudice* 7 (July/August 1973): 24–31.

Bernstein, Herman. *The History of a Lie: "The Protocols of the Wise Men of Zion." A Study.* New York, 1921.

———. *The Truth about "The Protocols of Zion": A Complete Exposure.* New York, 1935; 2d ed., 1971.

Burtsev, V. "*Protokoly Sionskikh Mudretsov" Dokazanny Podlog* ("The Protocols of the Elders of Zion" a proven forgery). Paris, 1938.

Charles, Pierre, S.J. *The Learned Elders of Zion.* New York, 1955.

——— *Les Protocoles des Sages de Sion.* Paris, 1938.

Cohn, Norman. *Warrant for Genocide: The Myth of the Jewish World Conspiracy and the Protocols of the Elders of Zion.* London, 1967; 2d ed., 1970.

Curtiss, John S. *An Appraisal of the Protocols of Zion.* New York, 1942.

Friedrich, Otto. *Die Weisen von Zion: Das Buch der Fälschungen.* Lübeck, 1920.

Graves, Philip. *The Truth about the Protocols: A Literary Forgery.* London, 1921.

Gwyer, John. *Portraits of Mean Men: A Short History of the Protocols of the Elders of Zion.* London, 1938.

Holmes, Colin. "New Light on the *Protocols of Zion.*" *Patterns of Prejudice* 11 (Nov./Dec. 1977): 13–21.

Institute of Jewish Affairs. *The Post-War Career of the Protocols of Zion.* Research Report. London, 1981.

Korey, William. *The Soviet "Protocols of the Elders of Zion": Anti-Semitic Propaganda in the U.S.S.R., August 1967–August 1977.* Washington DC, 1977.

Lachmann, F. R. "Die Protokolle der Weisen von Zion — Was Juden dazu sagen." *Jüdischer Presse Dienst* 1–3 (April 1987): 27–28.

Machover, J. M. *Dix ans aprés la chute de Hitler (1945–1955).* Paris, 1957.

Raas, E., and G. Brunschvig. *Vernichtung einer Fälschung: der Prozess um die erfundenen "Weisen von Zion."* Zurich, 1938.

Rollin, H. *L'Apocalypse de notre temps: les dessous de la propagande allemande d'après des documents inédits.* Paris, 1939.

Romano, Sergio. *I falsi protocolli: il "complotto ebraico" dalla Russia di Nicola II a oggi.* 2d ed. Milan, 1992.

Segel, Binjamin W. *Die Protokolle der Weisen von Zion, kritisch beleuchtet: Eine Erledigung.* Berlin, 1924.

Singerman, Robert. "The American Career of The Protocols of the Elders of Zion." *American Jewish History* (Sept. 1981): 48–78.

Spargo, John. *The Jew and American Ideals.* New York, 1921.

Spier, Howard. *Soviet Antisemitism Unchained: The Rise of the Historical and Patriotic Association: Pamyat.* Institute of Jewish Affairs Research Report. London, 1987.

Stein, Alexander. *Adolf Hitler Schüler der "Weisen von Zion."* Karlsbad, 1936.

Steinsbergowa, Aniela. "Protokoly Medrcow Syjona," *Krytyka* 15 (1983): 210–13.

Taguieff, Pierre-André. *Les Protocoles des Sages de Sion.* 2 vols. Paris, 1992.

U.S. Senate, Committee on the Judiciary. *A Report on a Forgery: The Protocols of the Learned Elders of Zion.* Washington DC, 1964.

Wolf, Lucien. *The Jewish Bogey and the Forged Protocols of the Learned Elders of Zion.* London, 1920.

WORKS OF RELATED INTEREST

Almog, Schmuel. *Antisemitism through the Ages.* New York, 1988.

Aronsfeld, C. C. *The Text of the Holocaust: A Study of the Nazis' Extermination Propaganda, 1919–1945.* Marblehead MA, 1985.

Bein, Alex. *Die Judenfrage: Biographie eines Weltproblem.* 2 vols. Stuttgart, 1980.

Besier, G. "Anti-Bolshevism and Antisemitism: The Catholic Church in Germany and National Socialist Ideology, 1936–37." *Journal of Ecclesiastical History* 43 (1992): 447–56.

Billig, Michael. "Rhetoric of the Conspiracy Theory: Arguments in National Front Propaganda." *Patterns of Prejudice* 22 (Summer 1988): 23–34.

Davis, D. B. "Some Theories of Counter-Subversion: An Analysis of Anti-Masonic, Anti-Catholic and Anti-Mormon Literature." In *Fear of Conspiracy*, edited by D. B. Davis. Ithaca NY, 1971.

Gilman, Sander L. *Jewish Self-Hatred: Anti-Semitism and the Hidden Language of the Jews.* Baltimore and London, 1986.

Katz, Jacob. *From Prejudice to Destruction: Anti-Semitism 1700–1933.* Cambridge MA, 1980.

———. *Jews and Freemasons in Europe, 1723–1939.* Cambridge MA, 1970.

Laqueur, Walter Z. *Russia and Germany: A Century of Conflict.* London, 1965.

Lebzelter, Gisela. *Political Antisemitism in England 1918–1939.* London, 1978.

Lee, Albert. *Henry Ford and the Jews.* New York, 1980.

Levy, Richard S., ed. *Antisemitism in the Modern World: An Anthology of Texts.* Lexington MA, 1991.

Lewis, Bernard. "The Arab World Discovers Anti-Semitism." *Commentary* 81 (May 1986): 30–34.

Pfahl-Traughber, Armin. *Der antisemitisch-antifreimaurische Verschwörungsmythos in der Weimarer Republik und im NS-Staat.* Vienna, 1993.

Roberts, John M. *The Mythology of the Secret Societies.* London, 1972.

Rogalla von Bieberstein, Johannes. *Die These von der Verschwörung 1776–1945: Philosophen, Freimaurerer, Juden, Liberale und Sozialisten als Verschwörer gegen die Sozialordnung.* Frankfurt am Main, 1976.

Rogger, Hans. *Jewish Policies and Right-Wing Politics in Imperial Russia.* London, 1986.

Rogger, Hans, and Eugen Weber, eds. *The European Right: A Historical Profile.* Berkeley, 1965.

Silbermann, Alphons, and J. H. Schoeps, eds. *Antisemitismus nach dem Holocaust: Bestandsaufnahme und Erscheinungsformen in Deutschsprächigen Ländern.* Köln, 1986.

Trachtenberg, Joshua. *The Devil and the Jews: The Medieval Conception of the Jew and Its Relation to Modern Anti-Semitism.* New Haven, 1943.

INDEX

Christian fundamentalists, and the *Protocols*, 26, 27
Christian National Crusade, 37
Churchill, Winston, 41
Cohn, Norman, 31
Coughlin, Father Charles E., 45 n.7
Czechoslovakia, 82, 103

Dearborn Independent, xii, 25–26, 63. *See also* Ford, Henry
Denikin, Anton Ivanovich, 77
Deutschvölkisch Schutz- und Trutzbund (German National Association for Offense and Defense), 23
Dialogue aux enfers entre Machiavel et Montesquieu, 123 n.15; excerpts, 99–101. *See also* Joly, Maurice
Douglas, Lord Alfred, 68, 86
Drumont, Edouard-Adolphe, 120 n.2, 127 n.30

Eastern Europe, Jews from, 13, 44, 45 n.3, 87
Ecuador, *Protocols* in, 35
Egypt, *Protocols* in, xiv, 36
Ehrenberg, Christian Gottfried, 117
El Salvador, *Protocols* in, 35
England. *See* Great Britain

Faisal, King, 36
Farrakhan, Louis, 39
Fauré, Félix, 103
Final Solution. *See* Holocaust
Ford, Henry: influence in Germany, 27–28, 63, 71; and *The International Jew*, xiii, 25, 63, 71; and the *Protocols*, xii, xv, 24–26, 63; recantation of antisemitism, 26–27
France, 53–55, 82, 84, 91, 125 n.24 n.25, 127 n.39; antisemitism in, 25, 54, 119 n.1, 120 n.2; Jews in, 125 n.24, 127 n.29 n.30; *Protocols* in, xi–xii, 3, 11, 14, 33, 52, 55, 62, 65, 68, 70–76, 84, 91, 97, 103;

Revolution (1789), 5, 9, 52–57, 81–82, 125 n.24; Revolution (1830), 54; Revolution (1848), 54
Frank, Leo, 24
Freemasons: and conspiracy, xiv, 21, 52–55, 57, 73–74, 77–80, 117, 122 n.11, 129 n.38; history of, 119 n.1; and Jews, xv, 53–54, 56, 59, 71, 74, 79, 91–92, 103, 106, 111, 123 n.14
Friedrich, Otto, 66–67, 94–95, 98
Fritsch, Theodor, xiii, 21, 27, 63, 70–71, 94, 112, 122 n.13; and Henry Ford, xiii, 27, 63

General Jewish Workers' Bund, 17
German National Association for Offense and Defense, 23
Germany, 18, 21–22, 33, 44, 51, 62, 64, 82, 84, 127 n.31; antisemitism in, 7, 13, 20–28, 32–33, 42–45, 69, 88, 116, 122 n.11 n.13, 123 n.19, 124 n.20, 127 n.31, 129 n.37; *The International Jew* in, xiii, 63; Jews in, 8, 21–23, 42–43, 77, 116; *Protocols* in, xii–xiv, 12, 20–33, 51, 60–64, 86; Revolution (1918), 22–23, 60, 64, 98
Ginsburg, Asher ("Ahad Ha'am"), 69, 124
gold standard, and Jews, 58–59
Goedsche, Hermann ("Sir John Retcliffe"), 55, 65–68; and *Biarritz*, 66, 95–99; "Rabbi's Speech," 46 n.12, 61, 66, 95–98
Gougenot des Mousseaux, Henri Roger, 54–55, 120 n.2
Graves, Philip, xiii, 67, 85, 128 n.35
Great Britain, 53, 58, 94; antisemitism in, xii, 41, 52; Jews in, 52; *Protocols* in, xii, 12, 33, 40–41, 63–65
The Great in the Small, xi, 60, 108, 114, 124 n.21. *See also* Nilus, Sergei
Greece, *Protocols* in, 33

Weishaupt, Adam, 120 n.1
Wichtl, Friedrich, 55–56, 120 n.4
Wilhelm II, Kaiser, 61, 122 n.11
Wilson, Woodrow, 29
Witte, Count Sergei, 103–6
World War I, 3, 20, 58, 121 n.5
World War II, 19, 29, 34
Wrangel, Baron Pyotr Niko-
laievich, 77

Zinoviev, Grigori, 18–19
Zionism, 18, 36, 42, 58, 112, 121 n.6,
124 n.19; and the *Protocols,* 71–80
Zionist congresses: Basel (1897),
60, 70–71, 78, 112, 121 n.9;
"Lwow" (1912), 61, 66–67;
Vienna (1925), 64
*Zionist Protocols. See Protocols of the
Elders of Zion*